VOL. 141

HAL•LEONARD
GUITAR
PLAY•ALONG

ACOUSTIC Hits

T0088293

ISBN 978-1-4584-0589-0

HAL•LEONARD®
CORPORATION

7777 W. BLUEMOUND RD. P.O. BOX 13819 MILWAUKEE, WI 53213

Visit Hal Leonard Online at
www.halleonard.com

VOL. 141

ACOUSTIC Hits

CONTENTS

GUITAR NOTATION LEGEND

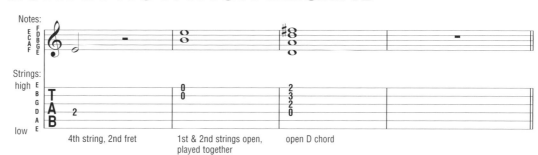

THE MUSICAL STAFF shows pitches and rhythms and is divided by bar lines into measures. Pitches are named after the first seven letters of the alphabet.

TABLATURE graphically represents the guitar fingerboard. Each horizontal line represents a string, and each number represents a fret.

4th string, 2nd fret   1st & 2nd strings open, played together   open D chord

HALF-STEP BEND: Strike the note and bend up 1/2 step.

WHOLE-STEP BEND: Strike the note and bend up one step.

GRACE NOTE BEND: Strike the note and immediately bend up as indicated.

SLIGHT (MICROTONE) BEND: Strike the note and bend up 1/4 step.

BEND AND RELEASE: Strike the note and bend up as indicated, then release back to the original note. Only the first note is struck.

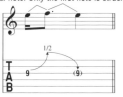

PRE-BEND: Bend the note as indicated, then strike it.

VIBRATO: The string is vibrated by rapidly bending and releasing the note with the fretting hand.

PALM MUTING: The note is partially muted by the pick hand lightly touching the string(s) just before the bridge.

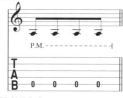

HAMMER-ON: Strike the first (lower) note with one finger, then sound the higher note (on the same string) with another finger by fretting it without picking.

PULL-OFF: Place both fingers on the notes to be sounded. Strike the first note and without picking, pull the finger off to sound the second (lower) note.

LEGATO SLIDE: Strike the first note and then slide the same fret-hand finger up or down to the second note. The second note is not struck.

SHIFT SLIDE: Same as legato slide, except the second note is struck.

TRILL: Very rapidly alternate between the notes indicated by continuously hammering on and pulling off.

TAPPING: Hammer ("tap") the fret indicated with the pick-hand index or middle finger and pull off to the note fretted by the fret hand.

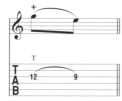

NATURAL HARMONIC: Strike the note while the fret-hand lightly touches the string directly over the fret indicated.

PINCH HARMONIC: The note is fretted normally and a harmonic is produced by adding the edge of the thumb or the tip of the index finger of the pick hand to the normal pick attack.

TREMOLO PICKING: The note is picked as rapidly and continuously as possible.

VIBRATO BAR DIVE AND RETURN: The pitch of the note or chord is dropped a specified number of steps (in rhythm), then returned to the original pitch.

VIBRATO BAR SCOOP: Depress the bar just before striking the note, then quickly release the bar.

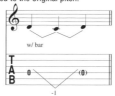

VIBRATO BAR DIP: Strike the note and then immediately drop a specified number of steps, then release back to the original pitch.

Additional Musical Definitions

(accent)   • Accentuate note (play it louder).

(staccato)   • Play the note short.

D.S. al Coda   • Go back to the sign (%), then play until the measure marked "*To Coda*," then skip to the section labelled "**Coda**."

D.C. al Fine   • Go back to the beginning of the song and play until the measure marked "*Fine*" (end).

Fill   • Label used to identify a brief melodic figure which is to be inserted into the arrangement.

N.C.   • Harmony is implied.

   • Repeat measures between signs.

• When a repeated section has different endings, play the first ending only the first time and the second ending only the second time.

Love Song

Words and Music by Jeffrey Keith and Frank Hannon

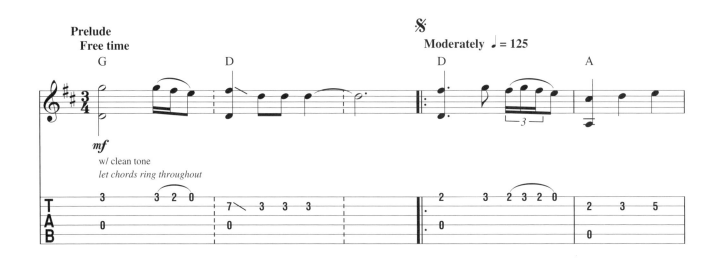

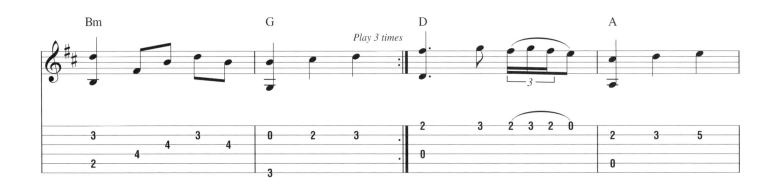

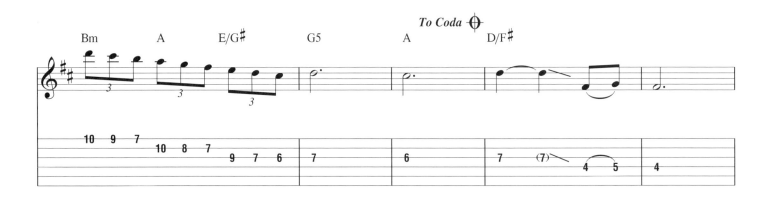

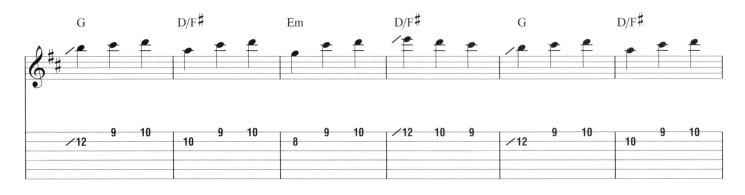

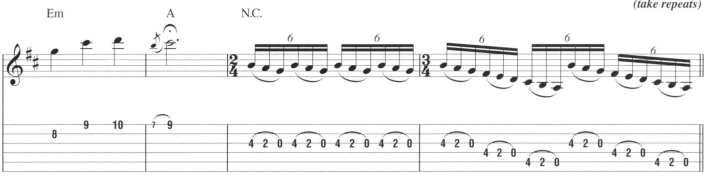

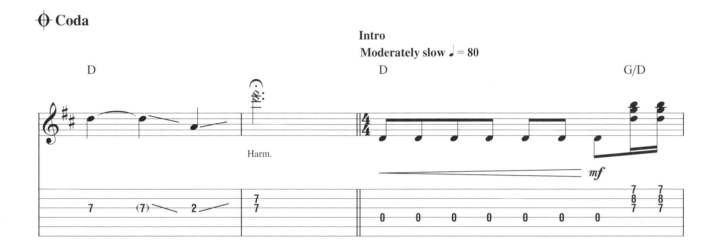

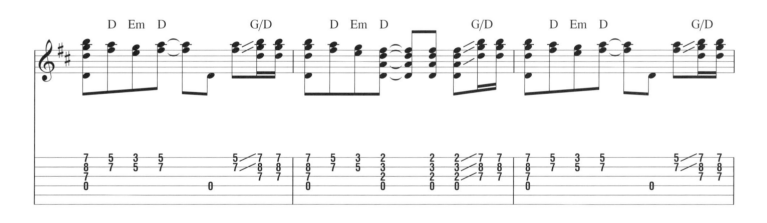

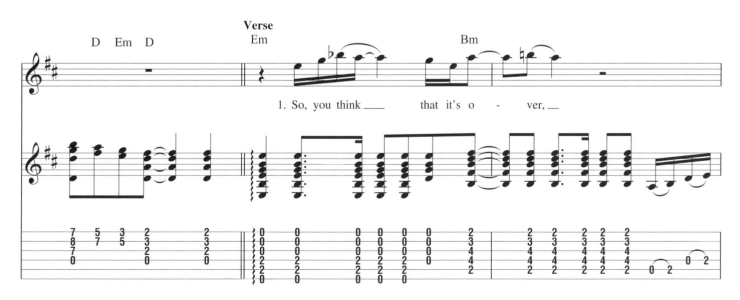

1. So, you think ____ that it's o - ver, ____

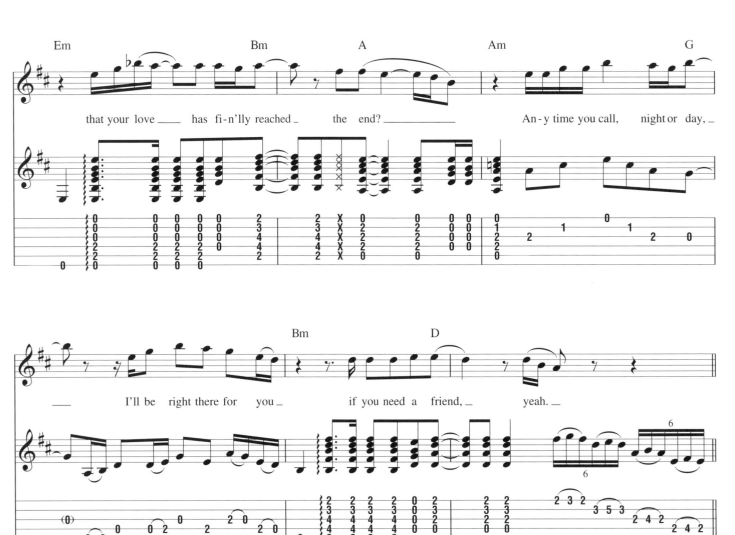

that your love ____ has fi-n'lly reached ____ the end? _____ An-y time you call, night or day, ___

____ I'll be right there for you ___ if you need a friend, ___ yeah. ___

Verse

2. It's gon-na take a lit-tle time. _____ Time is sure ___ to mend your bro-

-ken heart. _____ Don't ___ you e-ven wor-ry, pret-ty dar-lin', ___ 'cause

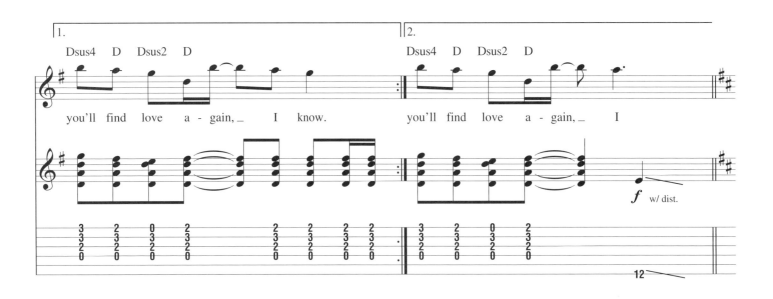

you'll find love a - gain, _ I know.   you'll find love a - gain, _ I

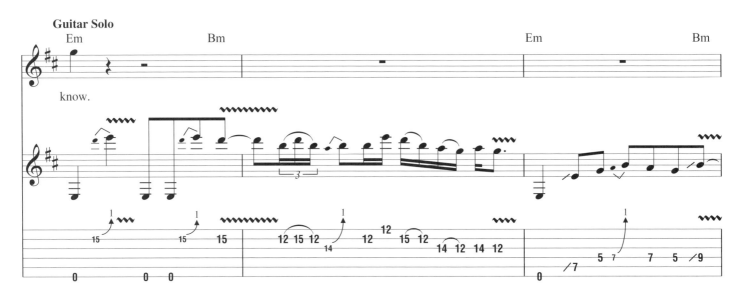

Guitar Solo

know.

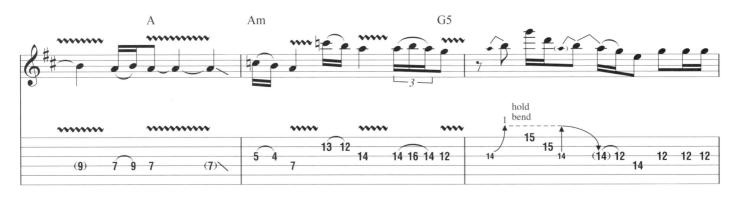

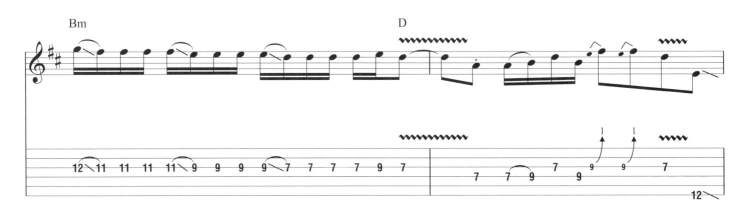

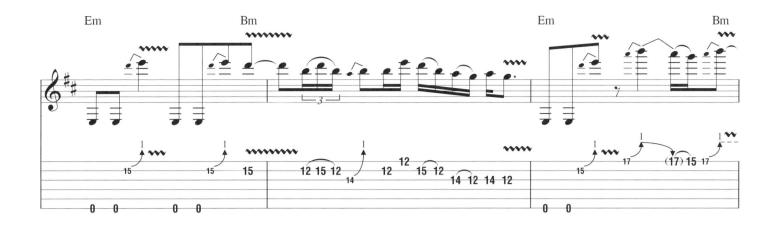

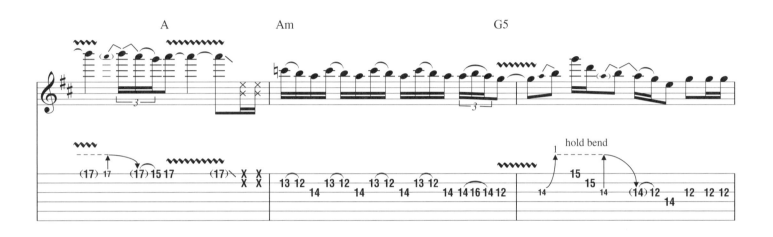

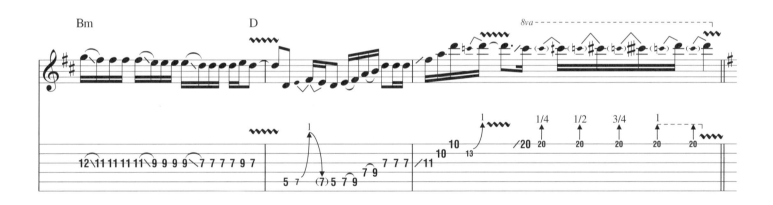

Chorus

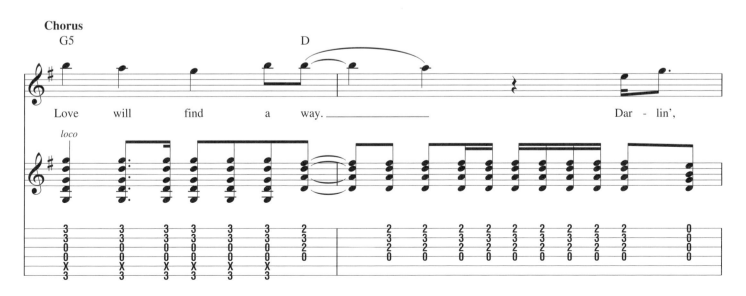

Love   will   find   a   way._____   Dar - lin',

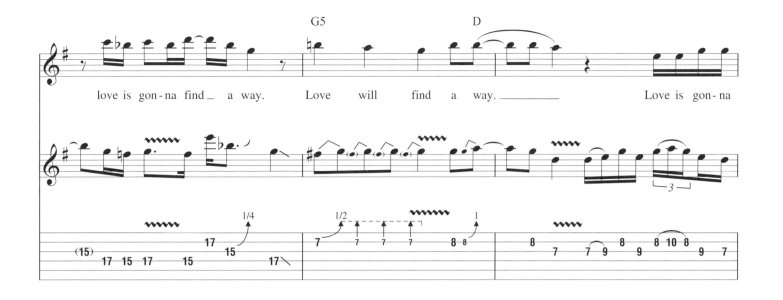

love is gon-na find _ a way.   Love   will   find   a   way. _____   Love is gon-na

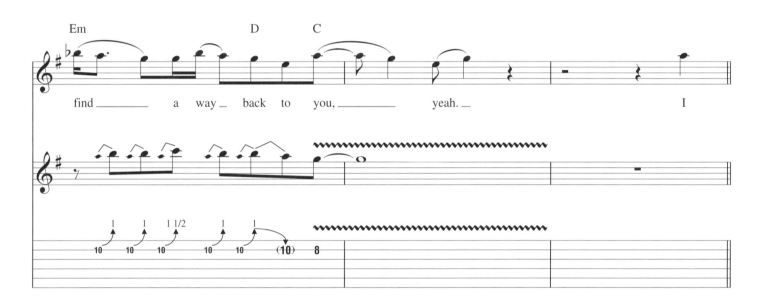

find _____   a way _ back to you, _____   yeah. _   I

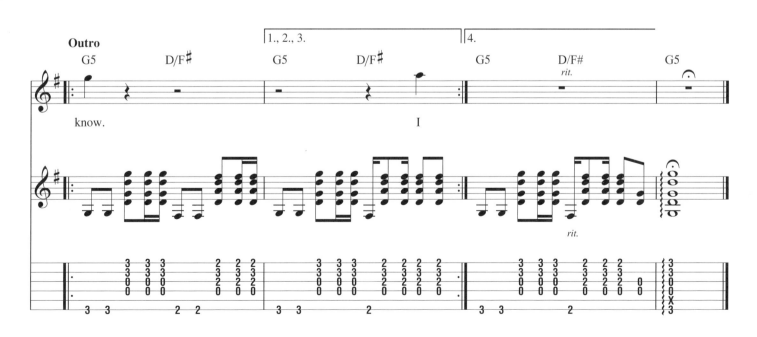

know.   I

Mr. Tambourine Man

Words and Music by Bob Dylan

Drop D tuning:
(low to high) D-A-D-G-B-E

Capo II

*Symbols in parentheses represent chord names respective to capoed guitar.
Symbols above represent actual sounding chords. Capoed fret is "0" in tab.

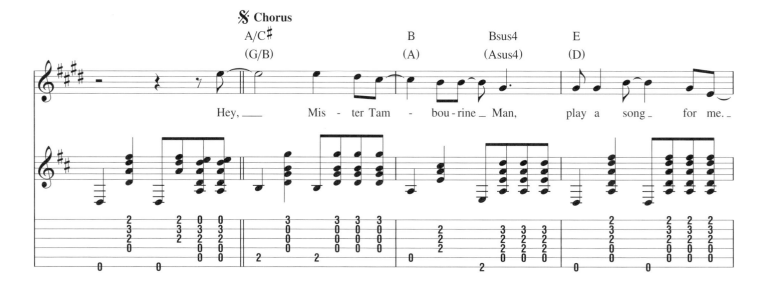

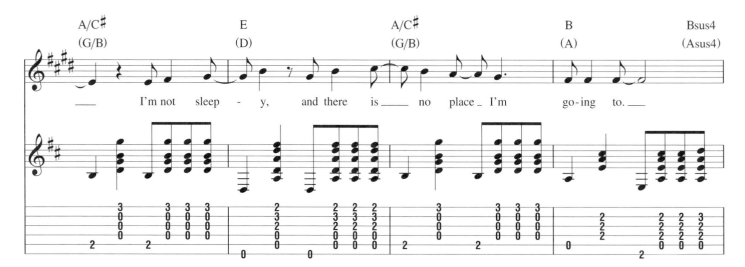

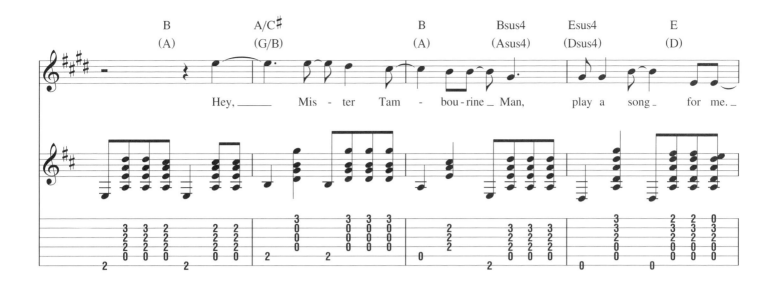

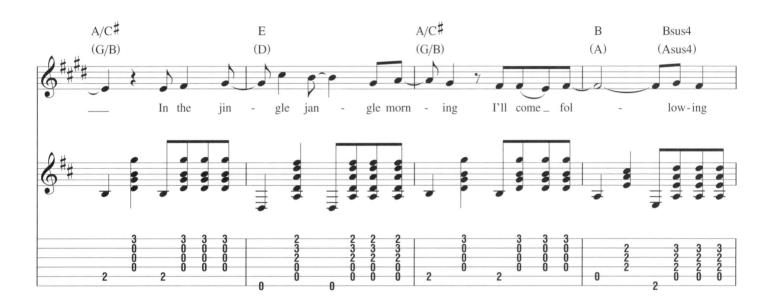

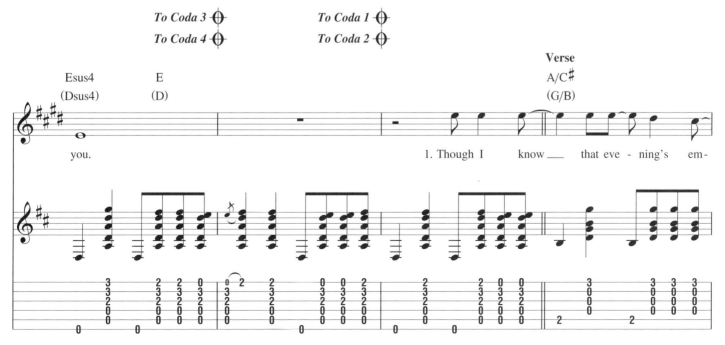

D.S. al Coda 2

20

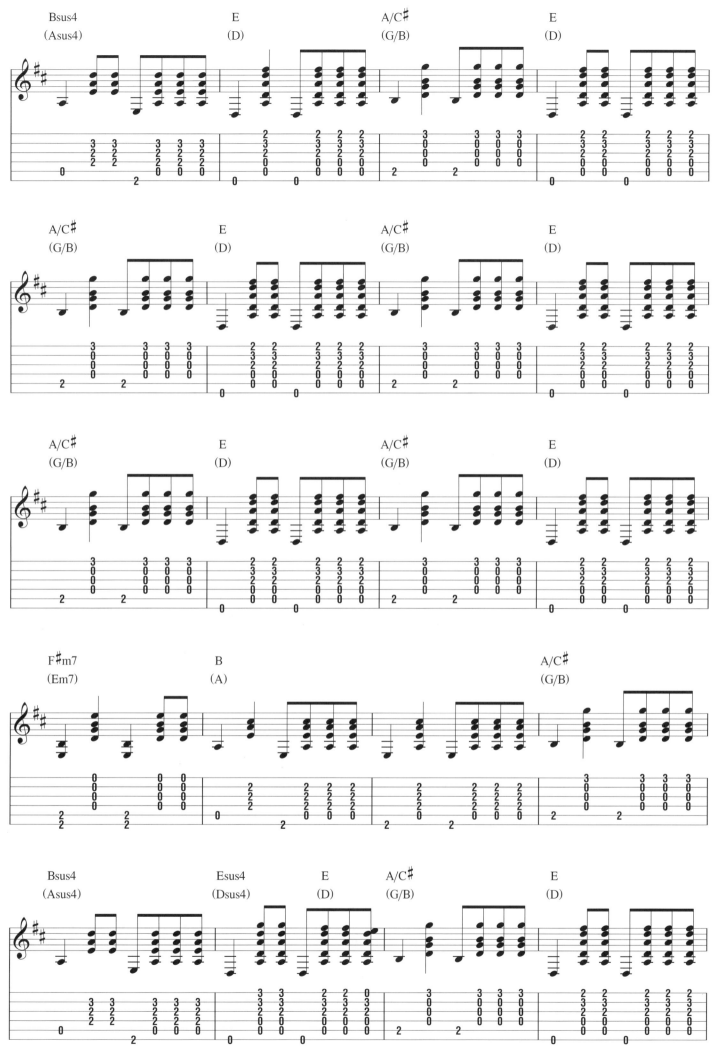

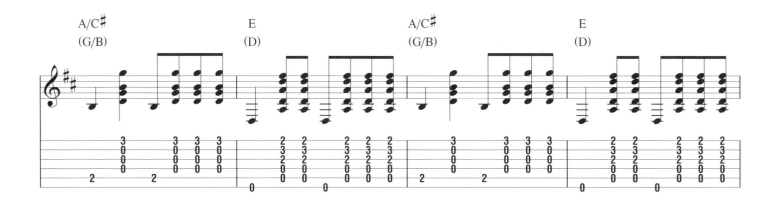

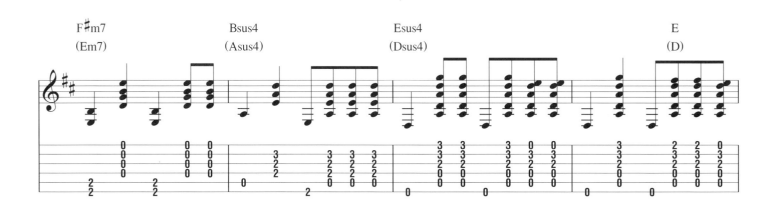

Verse

4. Then take ___ me dis - ap - pear - ing through the smoke ___

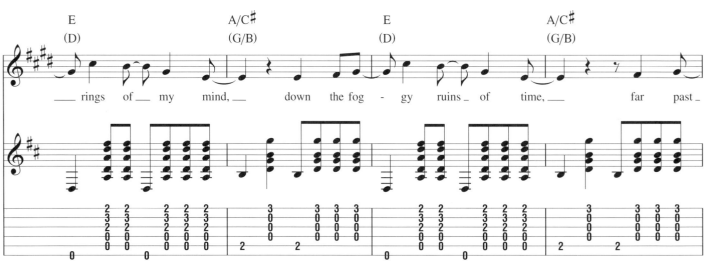

___ rings of ___ my mind, ___ down the fog - gy ruins ___ of time, ___ far past ___

Show Me the Way

Words and Music by Peter Frampton

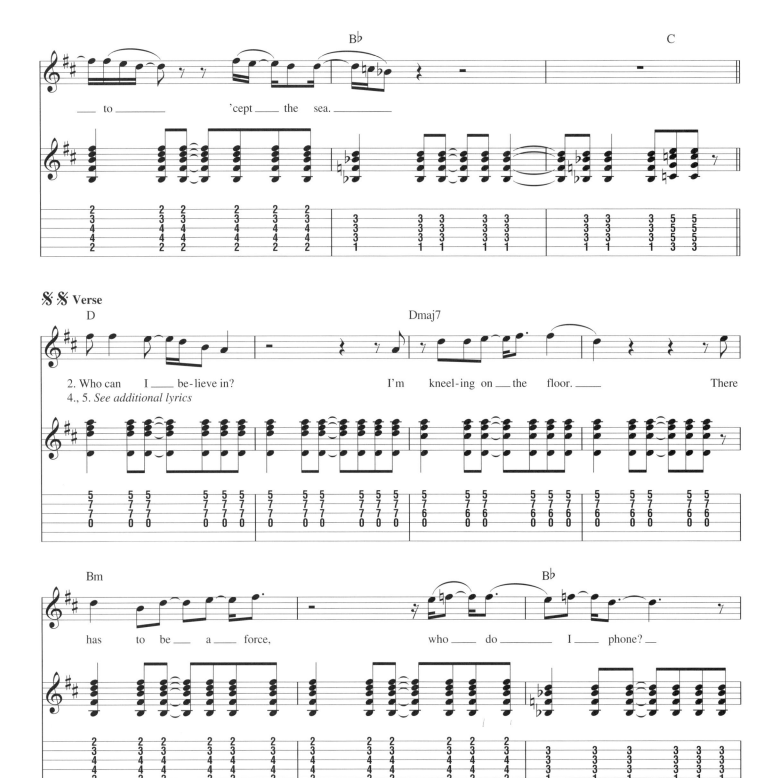

to ___ 'cept ___ the sea.

𝄋 𝄋 Verse

2. Who can I ___ be-lieve in? I'm kneel-ing on __ the floor. ___ There
4., 5. *See additional lyrics*

has to be a ___ force, who ___ do ___ I ___ phone? __

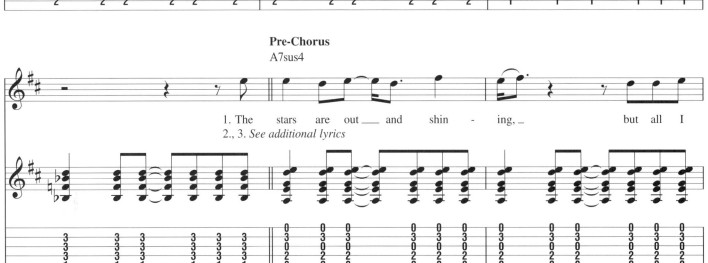

Pre-Chorus

1. The stars are out ___ and shin - ing, __ but all I
2., 3. *See additional lyrics*

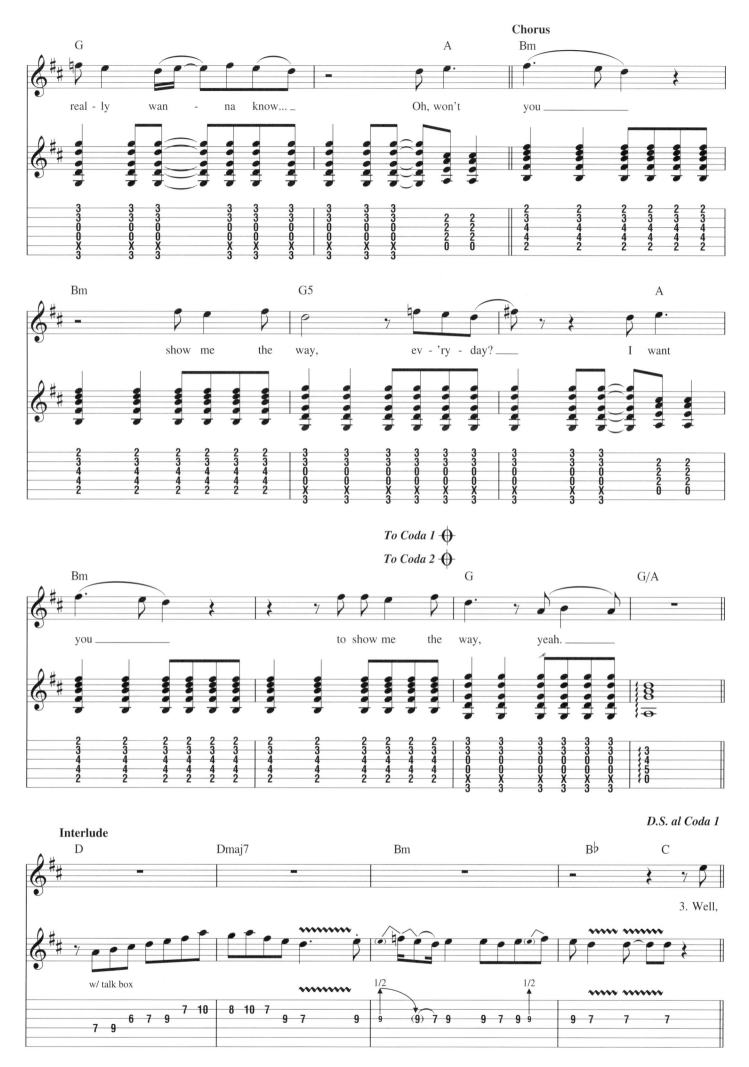

⊕ Coda 1

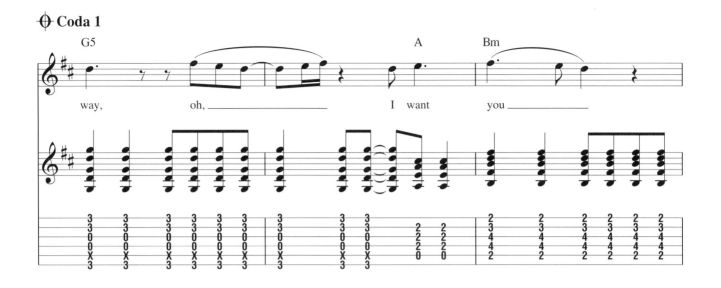

way, oh, _____ I want you _____

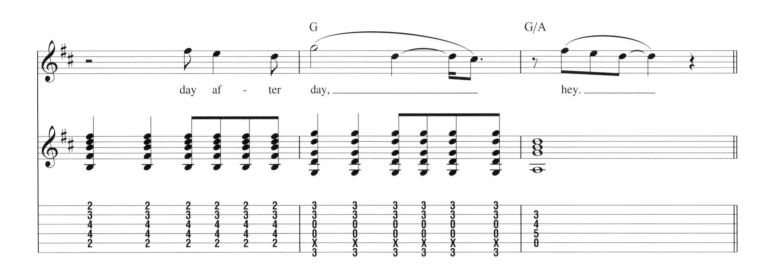

day af- ter day, _____ hey. _____

Guitar Solo

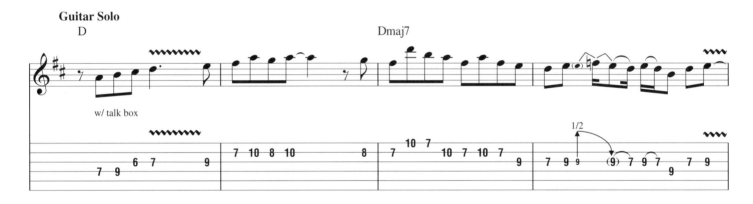

w/ talk box

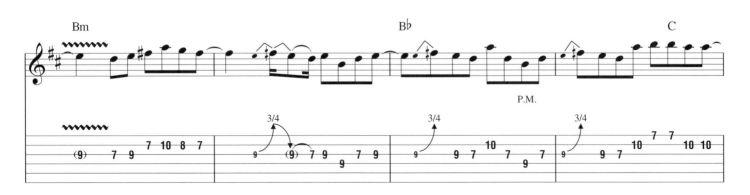

28

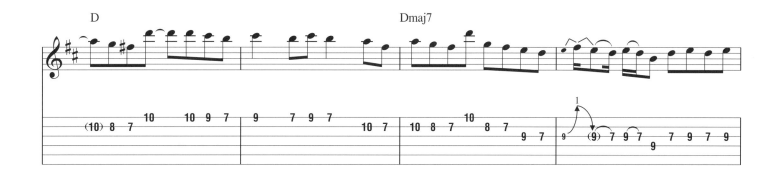

D.S.S. al Coda 2

5. An', __ I

⊕ Coda 2

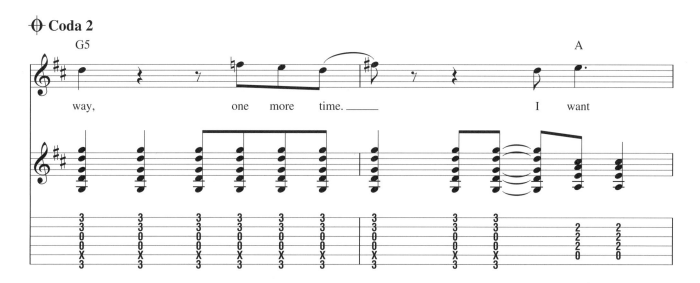

way,   one more time. _____   I want

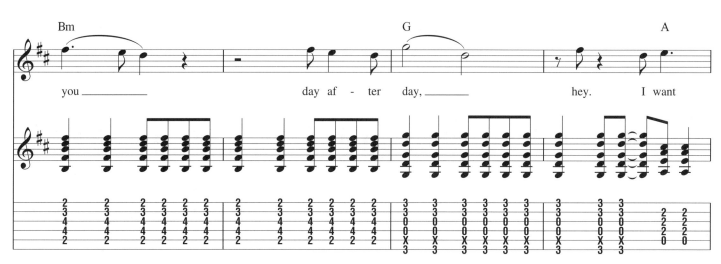

you _____   day af - ter day, _____   hey. I want

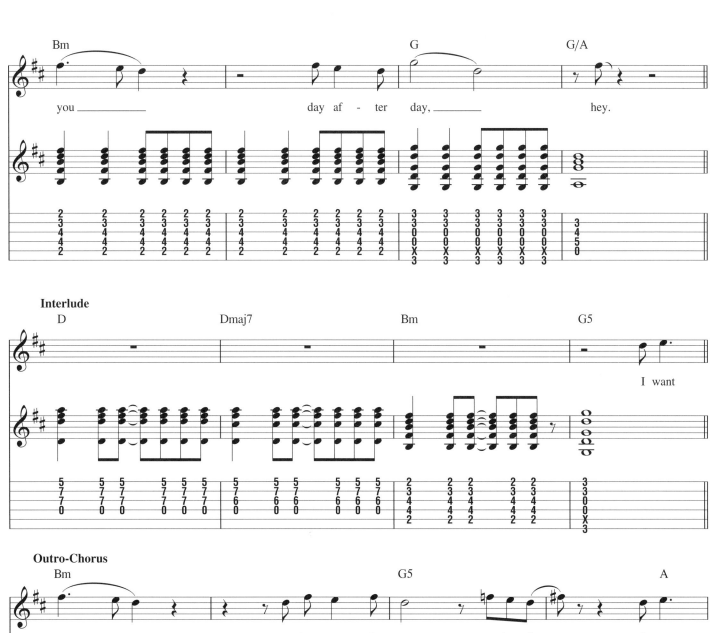

Interlude

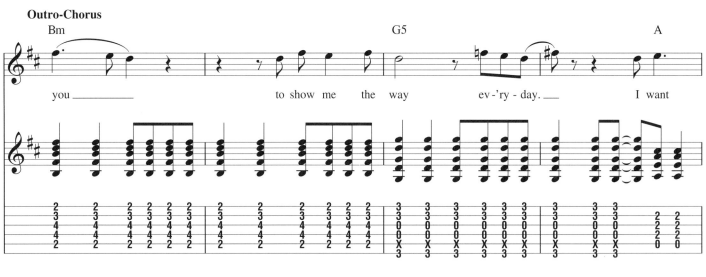

Outro-Chorus

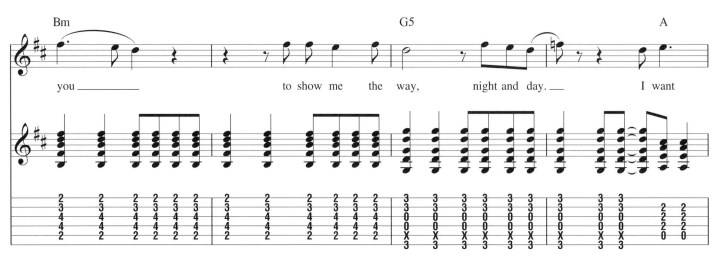

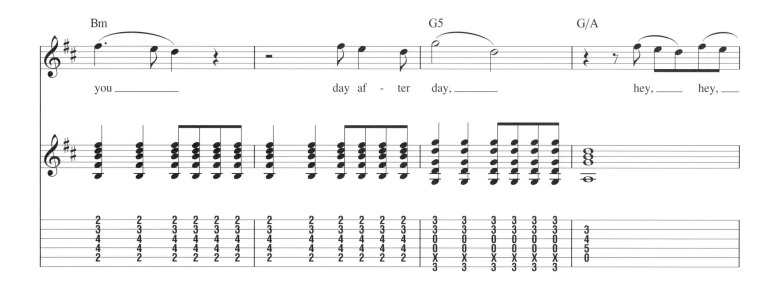

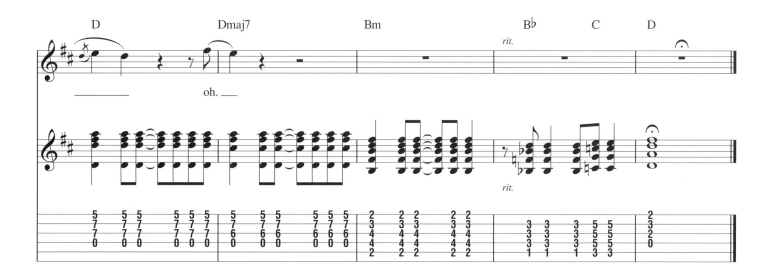

Additional Lyrics

3. Well, I can see no reason,
   You living on your nerves,
   When someone drops a cup
   And I submerge.

4. I'm swimming in a circle,
   I feel I'm going down.
   There has to be a fool
   To play my part.

Pre-Chorus 2. Well, someone thought of healing
   But all I really wanna know...

5. An' I wonder if I'm dreaming,
   I feel so unashamed.
   I can't believe this is happening
   To me.

Pre-Chorus 3. I watch you when you're sleeping,
   Oh, then I wanna take your love...

The Sound of Silence

Words and Music by Paul Simon

Capo VI

Verse
Moderately ♩ = 104

*Chord symbols in parentheses represent chord names respective to capoed guitar.
Symbols above reflect actual sounding chords. Capoed fret is "0" in tab.

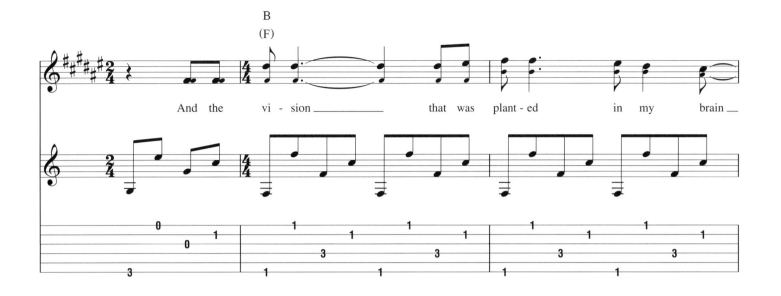

And the vi - sion _____ that was plant - ed in my brain _____

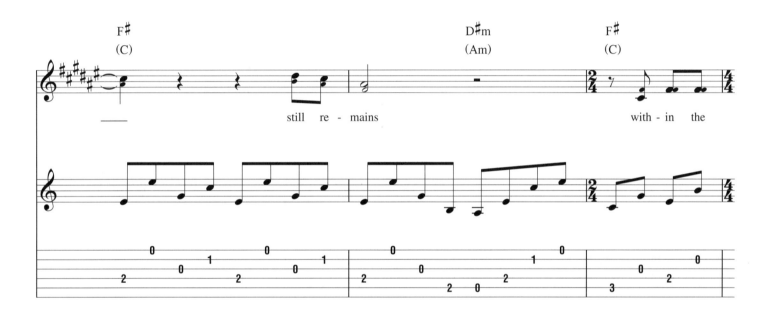

B
(F)

F#
(C)

D#m
(Am)

F#
(C)

_____ still re - mains with - in the

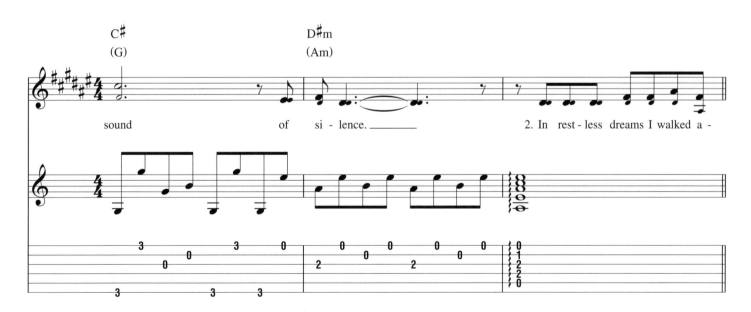

C#
(G)

D#m
(Am)

sound of si - lence. _____ 2. In rest - less dreams I walked a -

Verse

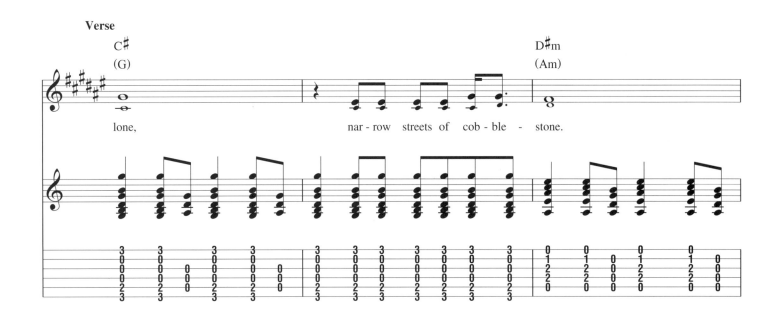

lone,　　　nar - row streets of cob - ble - stone.

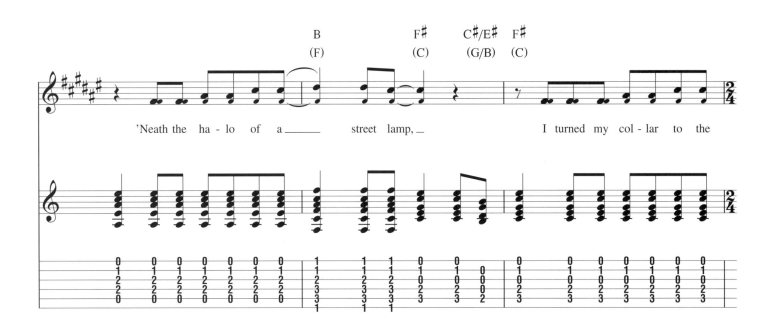

'Neath the ha - lo of a＿＿ street lamp,＿　　I turned my col - lar to the

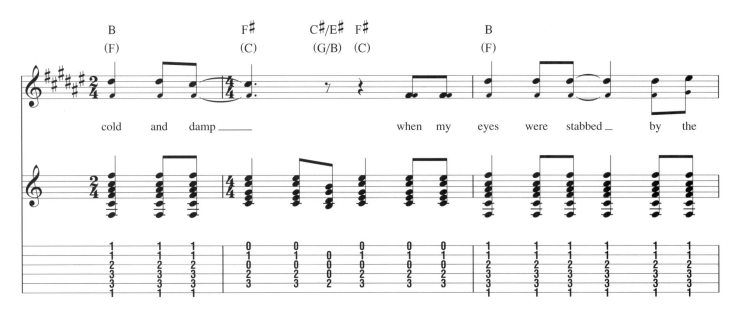

cold　　and　damp＿＿＿　　when my eyes were stabbed ＿ by the

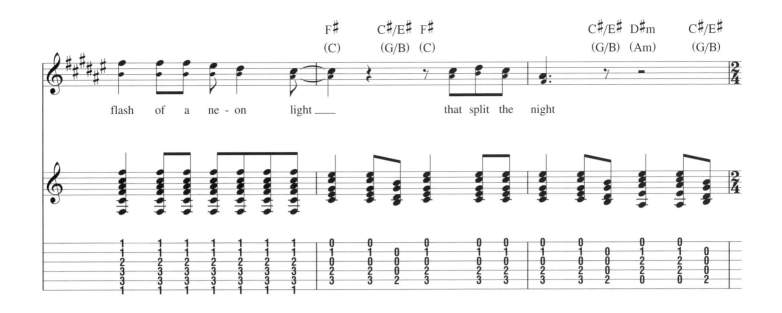

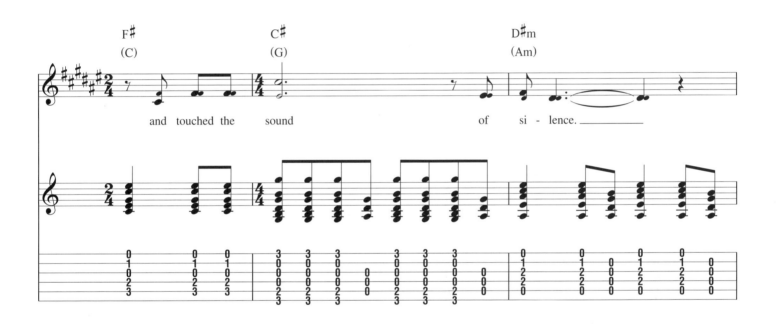

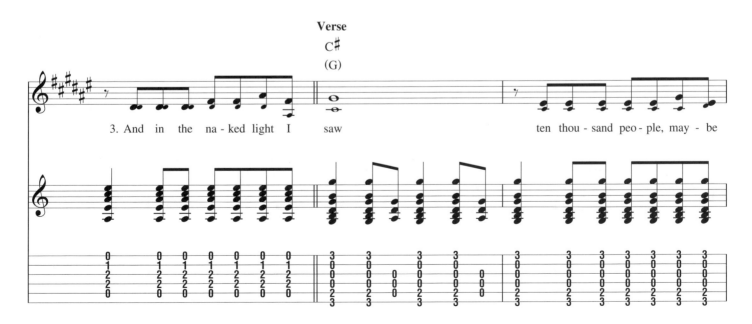

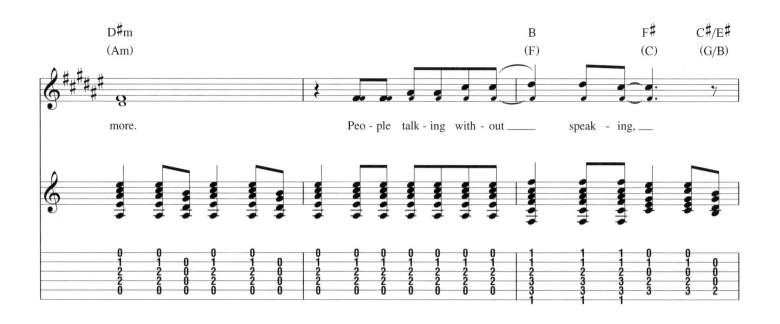

more.   Peo - ple talk - ing with - out _____ speak - ing, _____

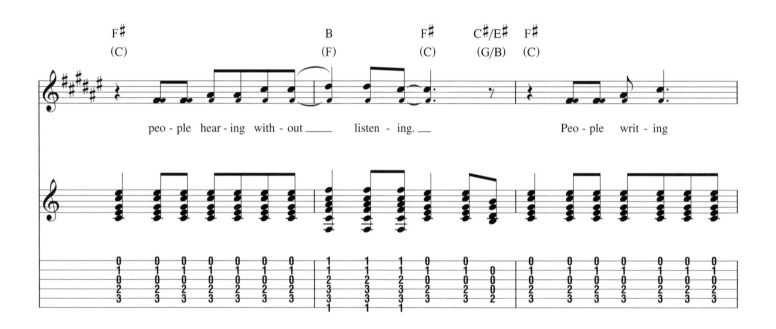

peo - ple hear - ing with - out _____ listen - ing. _____   Peo - ple writ - ing

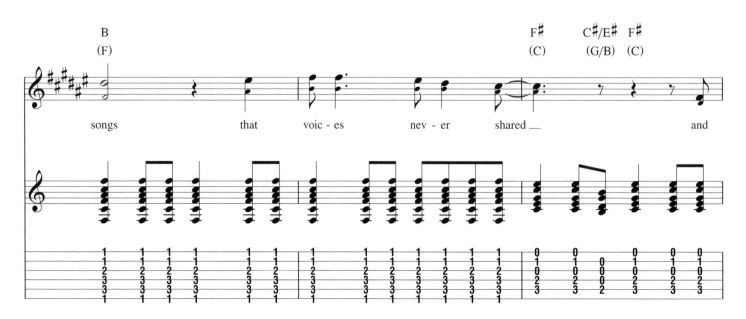

songs   that   voic - es   nev - er   shared ____   and

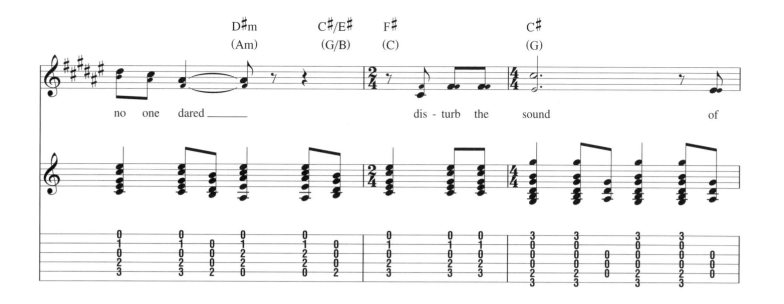

no one dared _____ dis - turb the sound of

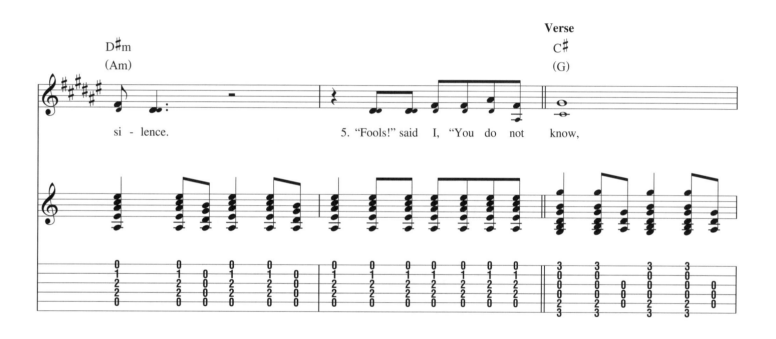

si - lence. 5. "Fools!" said I, "You do not know,

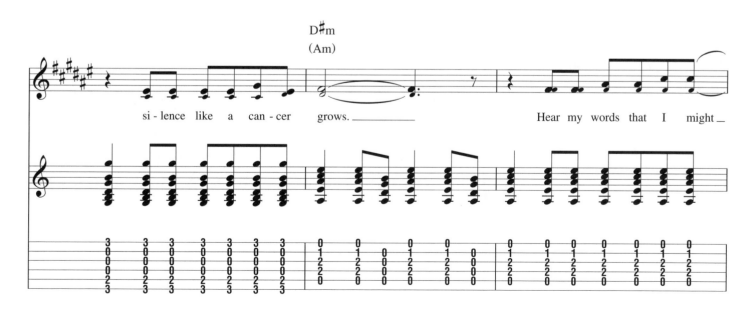

si - lence like a can - cer grows. _____ Hear my words that I might __

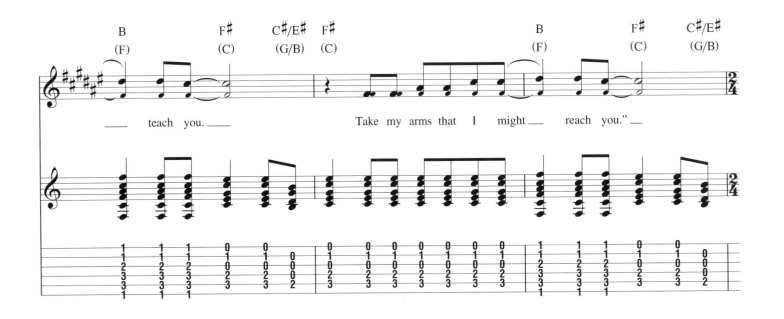

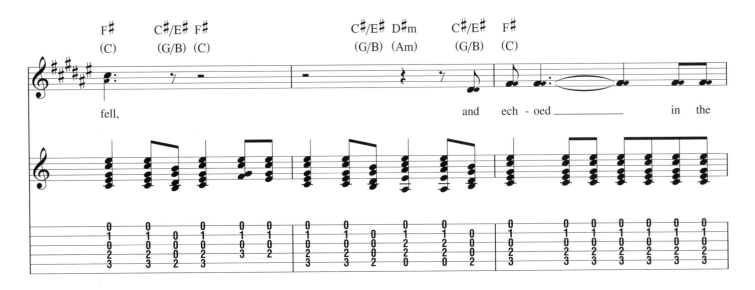

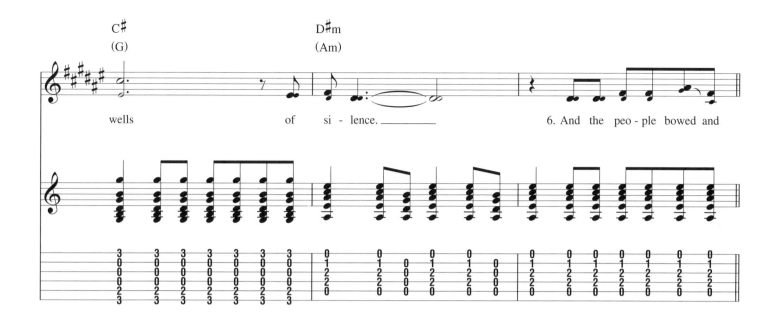

wells of si-lence._____ 6. And the peo-ple bowed and

Verse

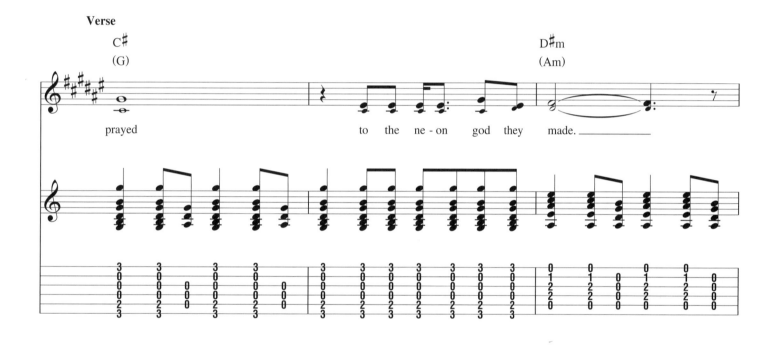

prayed to the ne-on god they made._____

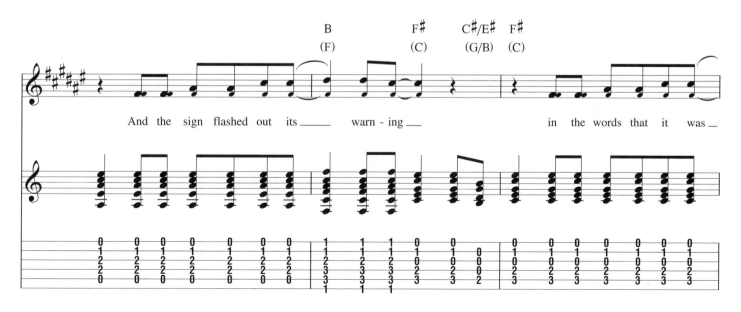

And the sign flashed out its_____ warn-ing_____ in the words that it was_____

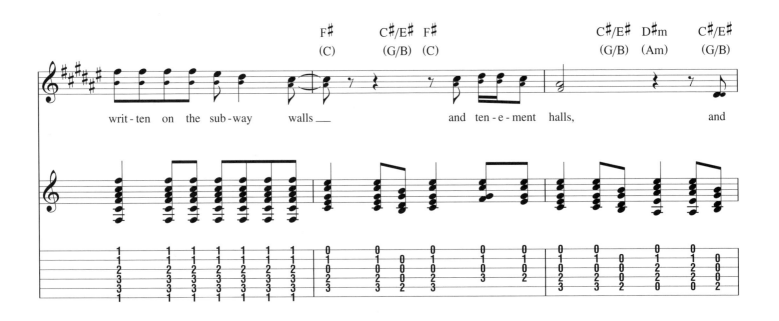

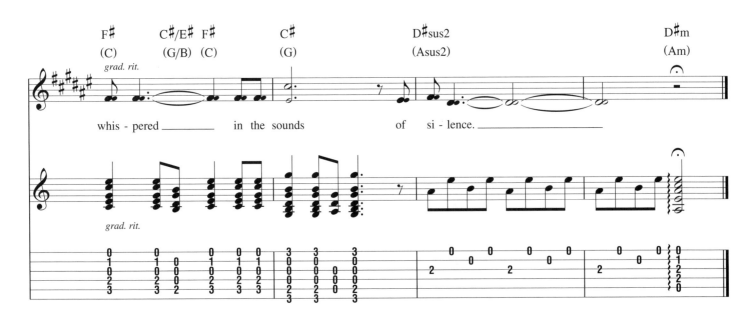

Southern Cross

Words and Music by Stephen Stills, Richard Curtis and Michael Curtis

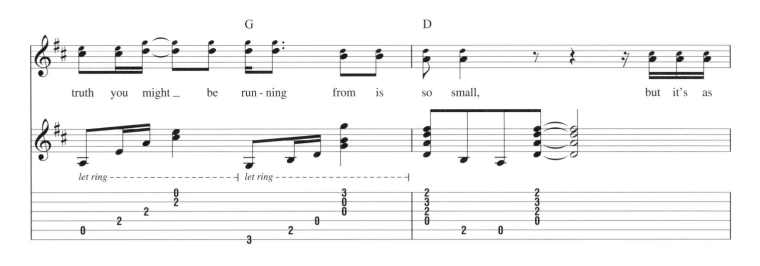

truth you might _ be run-ning from is so small, but it's as

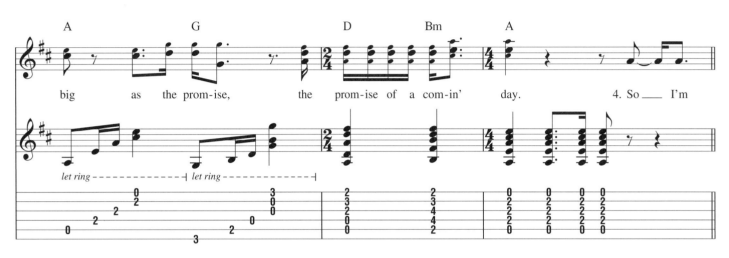

big as the prom-ise, the prom-ise of a com-in' day. 4. So _ I'm

Verse

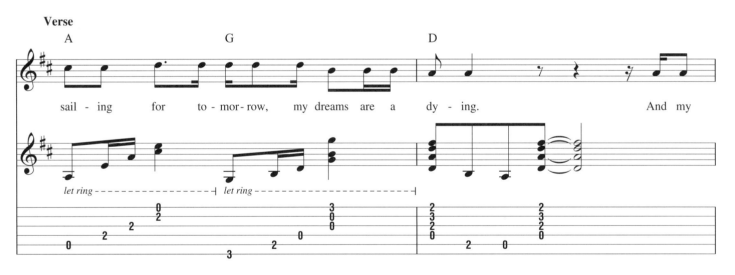

sail-ing for to-mor-row, my dreams are a dy-ing. And my

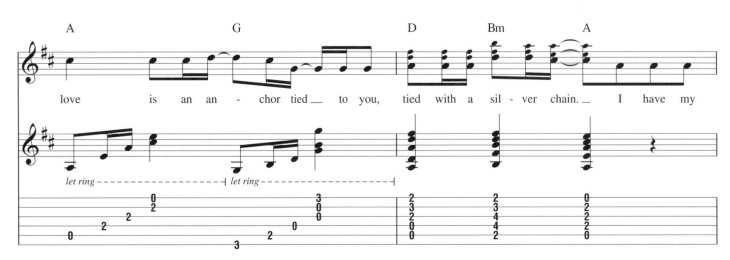

love is an an-chor tied _ to you, tied with a sil-ver chain. _ I have my

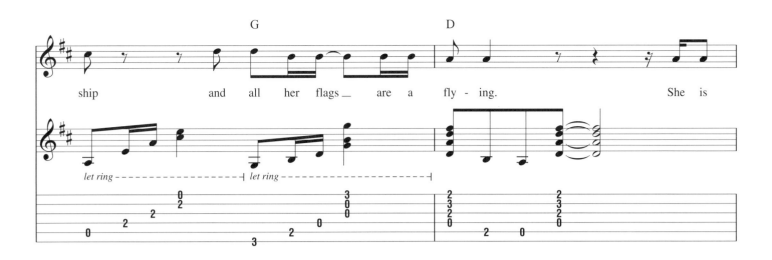

ship and all her flags ___ are a fly - ing. She is

let ring - - - - - - - - - - - - *let ring* - - - - - - - - - - - - - - - -

D.S. al Coda

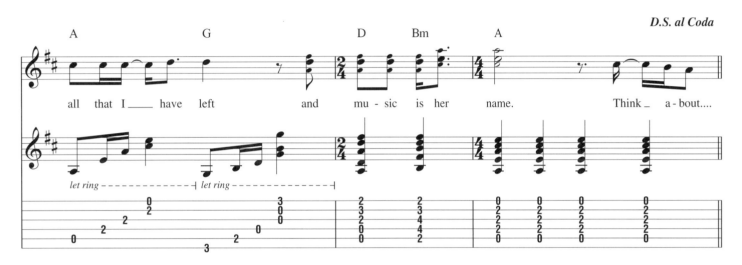

all that I ___ have left and mu - sic is her name. Think ___ a - bout....

let ring - - - - - - - - - - - - *let ring* - - - - - - - - - - - -

⊕ **Coda**

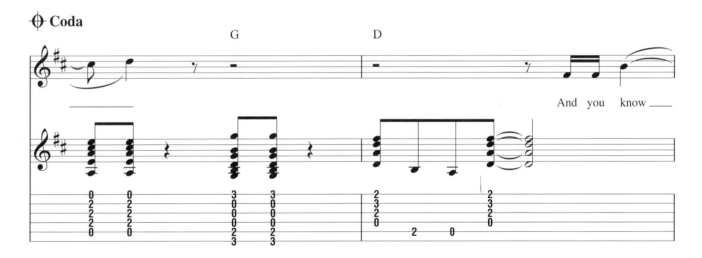

And you know ___

_____

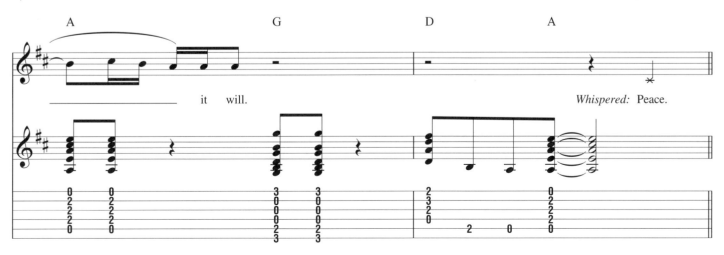

_____ it will. *Whispered:* Peace.

Interlude

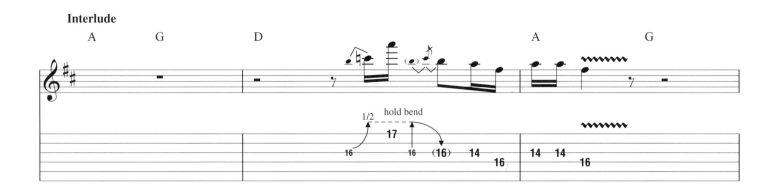

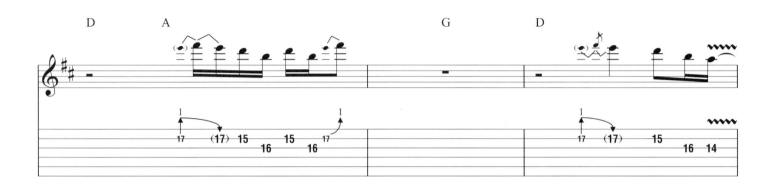

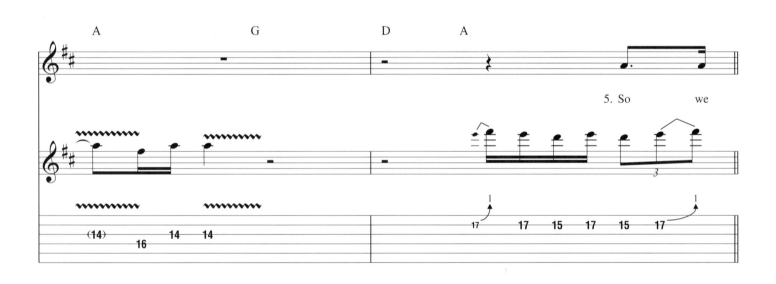

5. So we

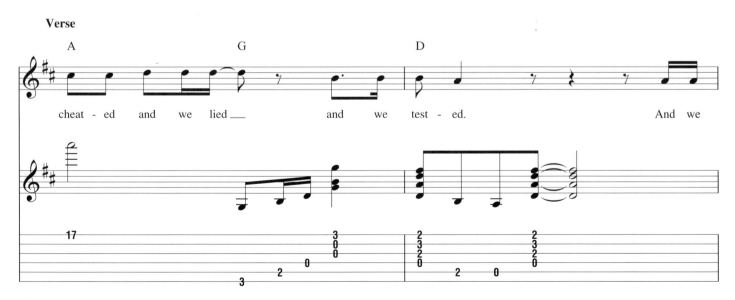

Verse

cheat - ed and we lied ___ and we test - ed. And we

Who'll Stop the Rain

Words and Music by John Fogerty

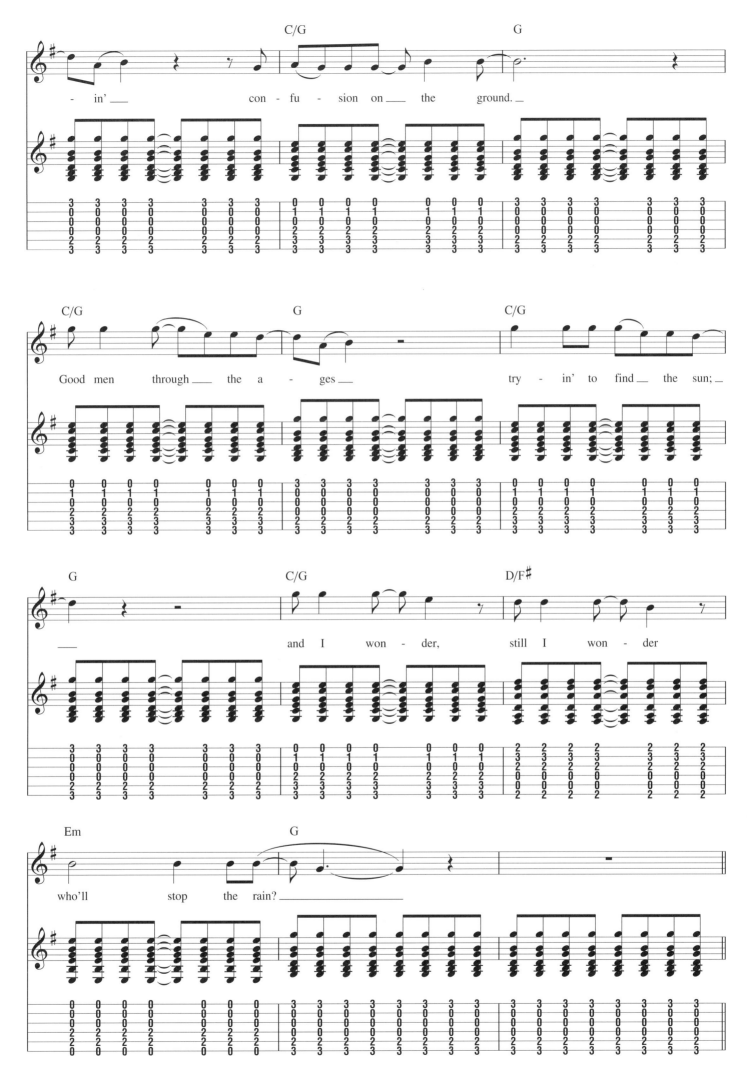

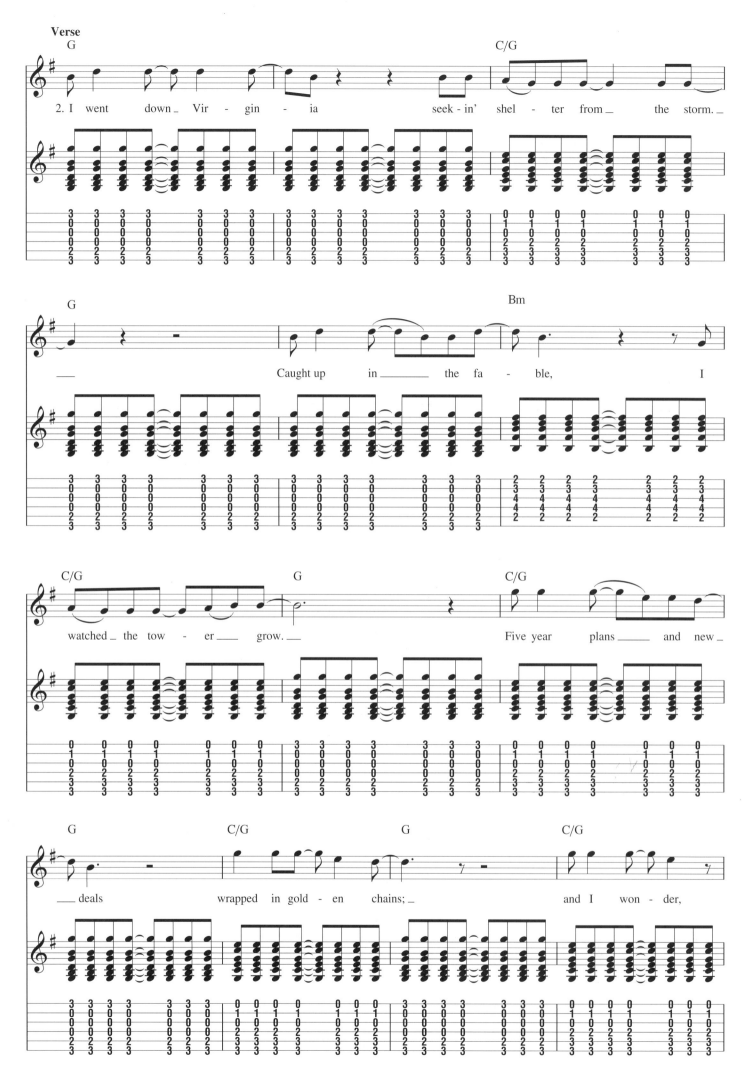

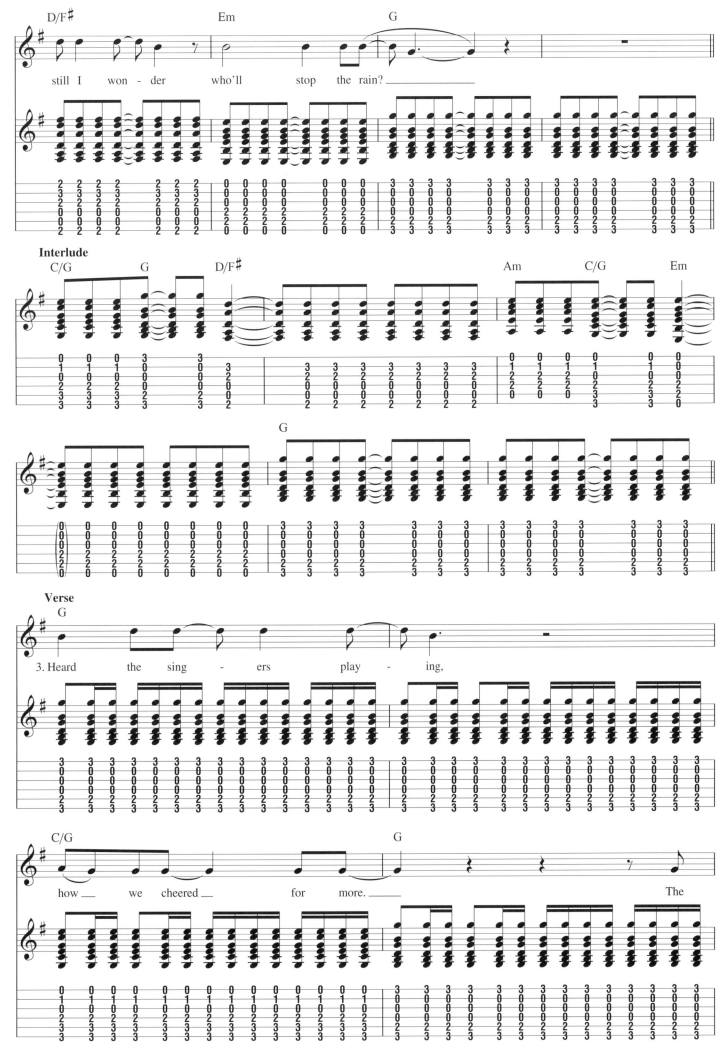

crowd had rushed __ to - geth - er, try - in' to __ keep warm. __

Still the rain __ kept pour - in', fall - in' on __ my ears; __

and I won - der, still I won - der who'll stop the rain? _____

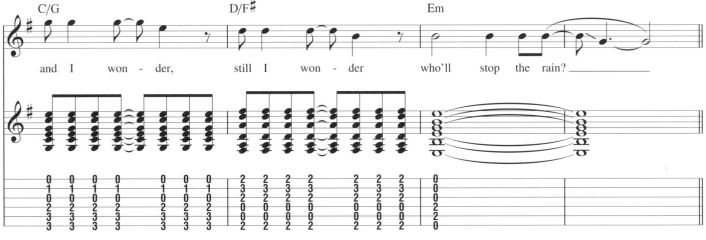

Repeat and fade

Outro

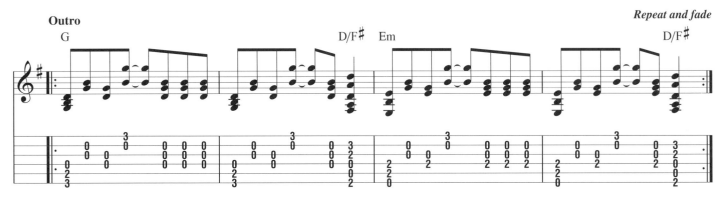

Wonderwall

Words and Music by Noel Gallagher

Capo II

Intro
Moderately ♩ = 87

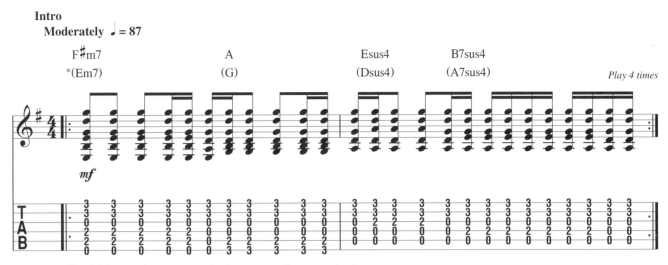

Play 4 times

*Symbols in parentheses represent chord names respective to capoed guitar.
Symbols above reflect actual sounding chords. Capoed fret is "0" in tab.

Verse

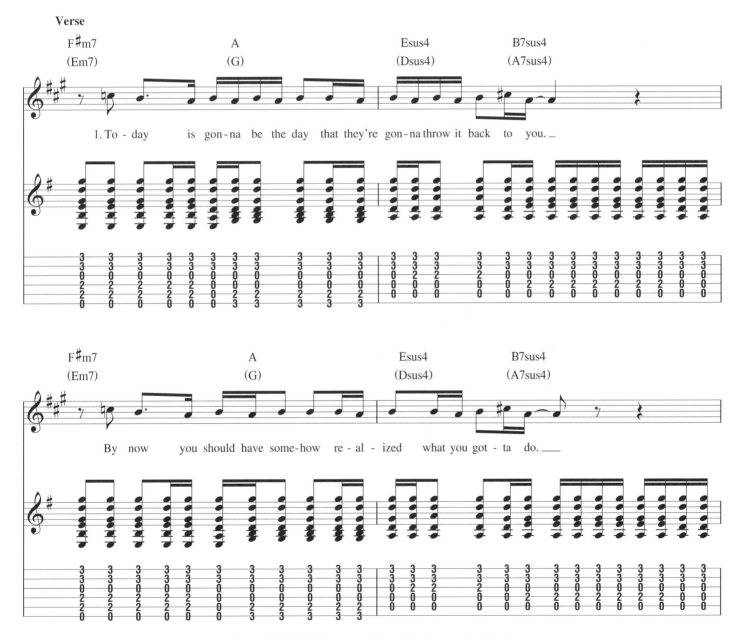

1. To-day is gon-na be the day that they're gon-na throw it back to you. _

By now you should have some-how re-al-ized what you got-ta do. _

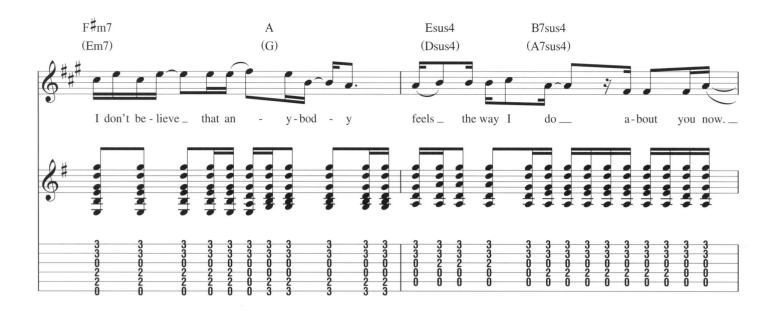

I don't be-lieve _ that an - y-bod - y feels _ the way I do _ a-bout you now. _

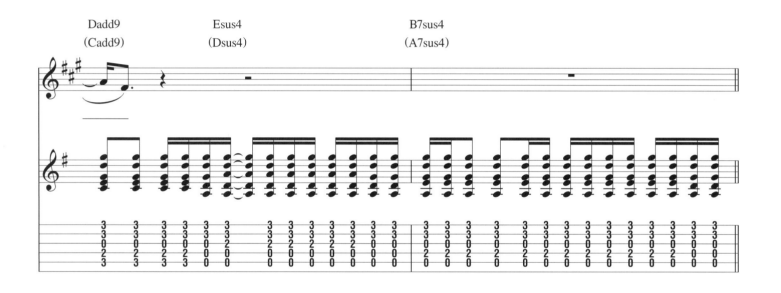

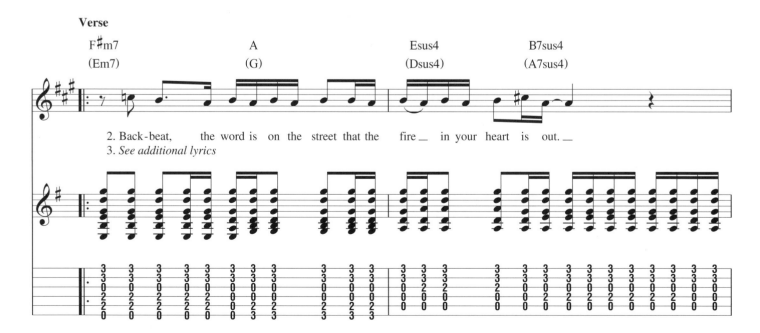

Verse

2. Back-beat, the word is on the street that the fire _ in your heart is out. _
3. *See additional lyrics*

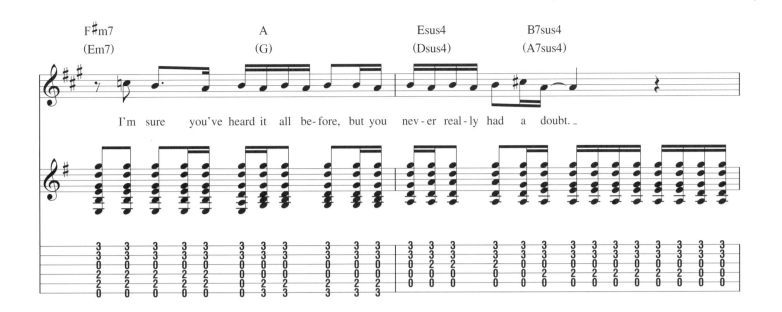

I'm sure you've heard it all be-fore, but you nev-er real-ly had a doubt.

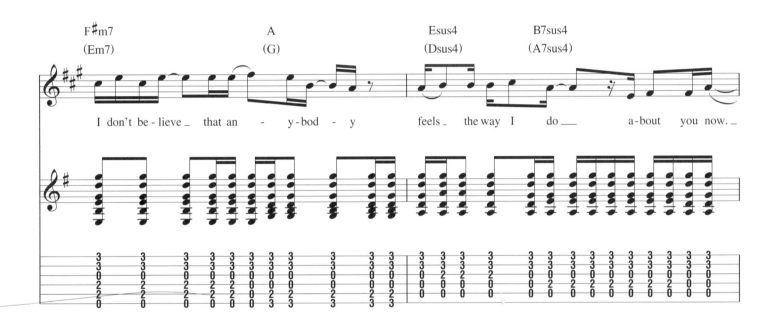

I don't be-lieve _ that an - y-bod - y feels _ the way I do __ a-bout you now. _

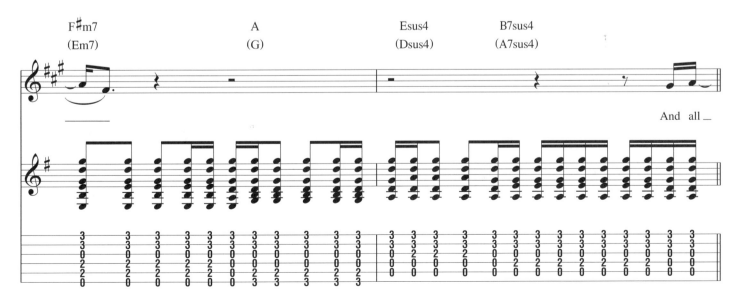

_____ And all _

Pre-Chorus

the roads _ we have _ to walk _ are wind - ing, and all _

See additional lyrics

let chords ring throughout

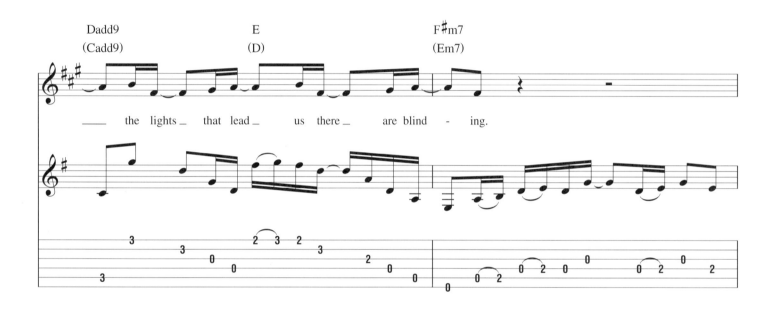

the lights _ that lead _ us there _ are blind - ing.

There are man - y things _ that I ___ would like to say to you, _ but I don't know how _

Be - cause

Chorus

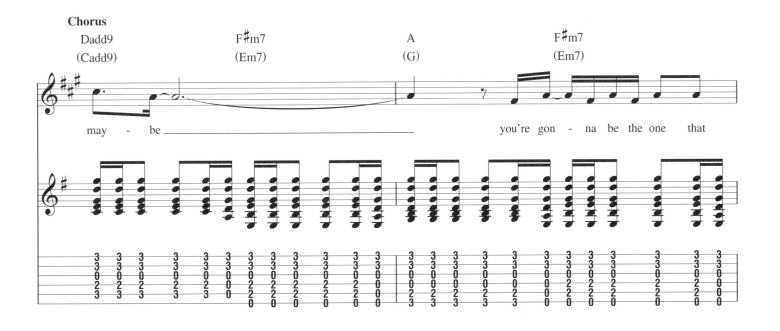

may - be _____ you're gon - na be the one that

saves __ me. _____ And af - ter all _____

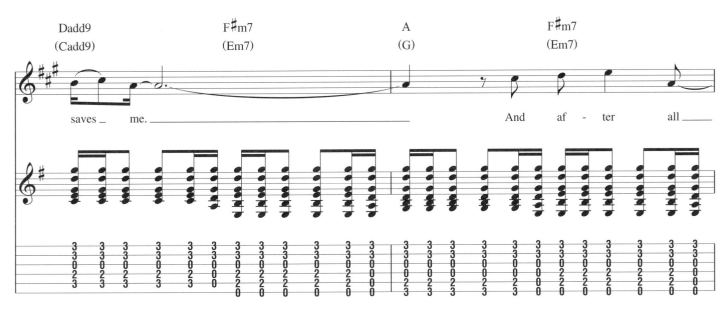

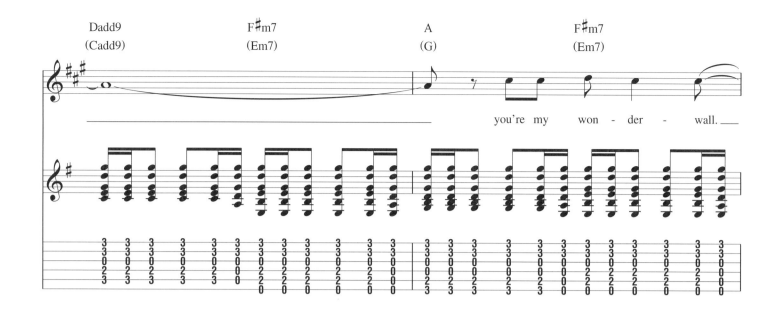

you're my won - der - wall. _____

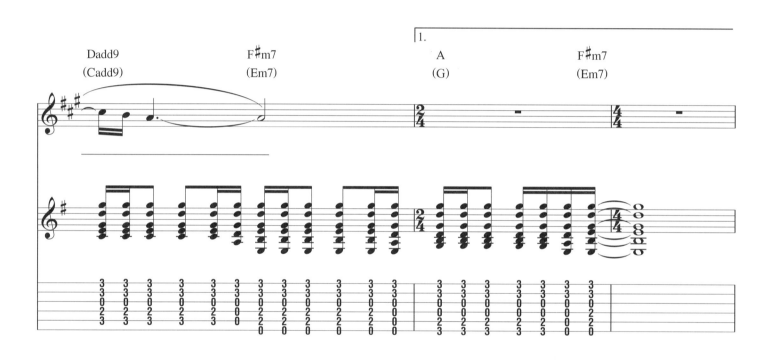

I said

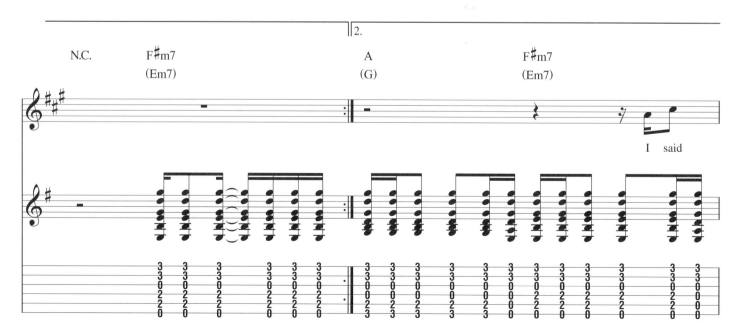

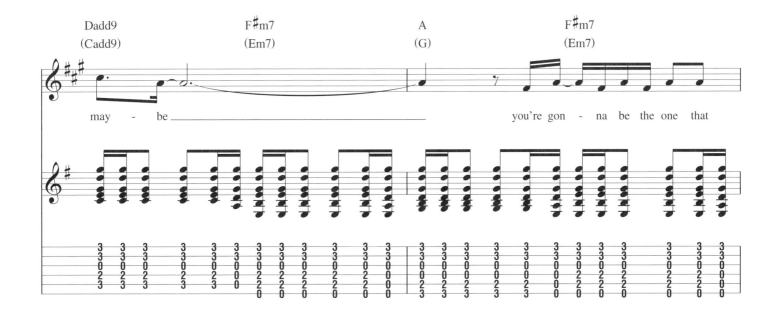

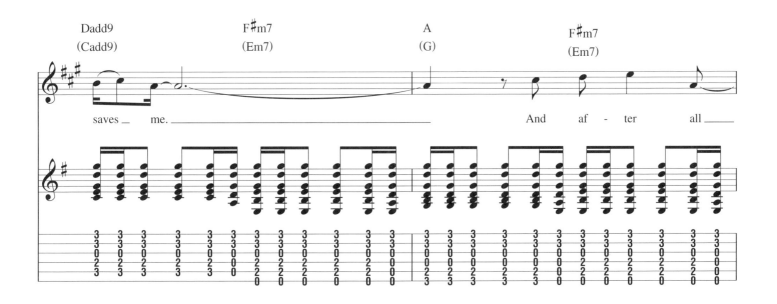

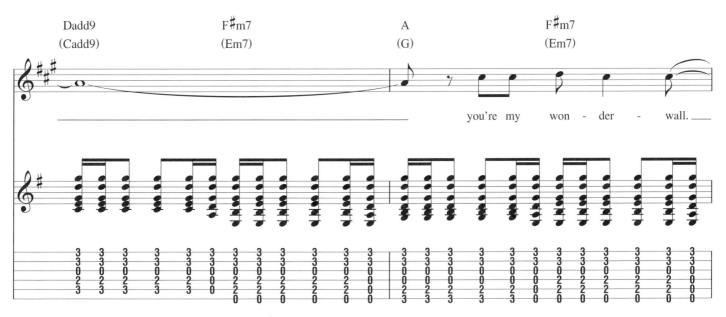

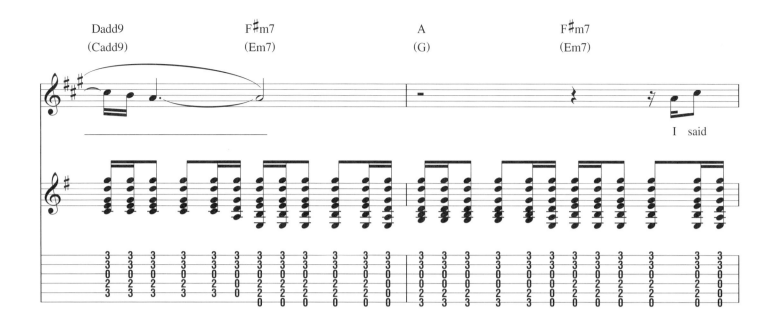

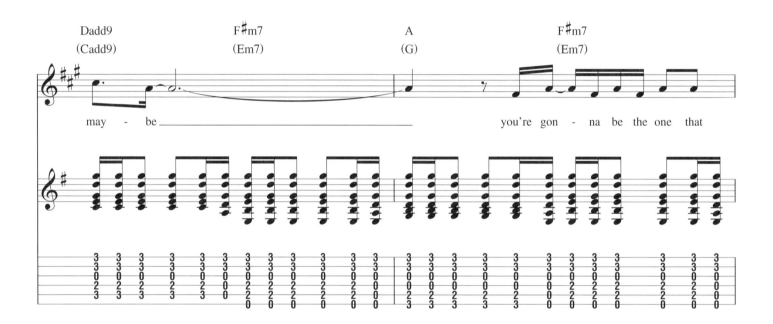

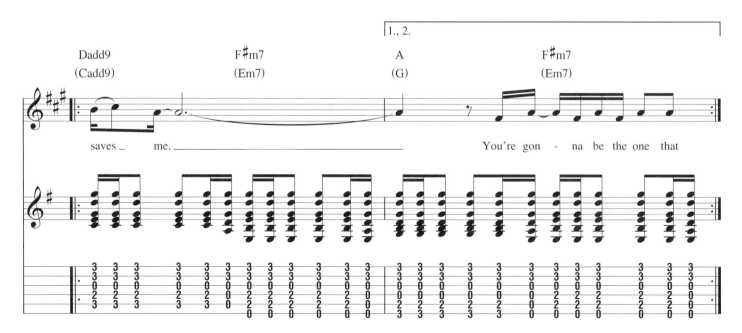

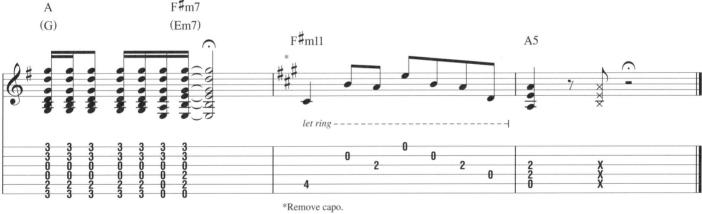

*Remove capo.

Additional Lyrics

2. Today was gonna be the day, but they'll never throw it back to you.
By now you should have somehow realized what you're not to do.
I don't believe that anybody feels the way I do about you now.

Pre-Chorus 2. And all the roads that lead you there were winding,
And all the lights that light the way are blinding.
There are many things that I would like to say to you,
But I don't know how.
I said...

Wild World

Words and Music by Cat Stevens

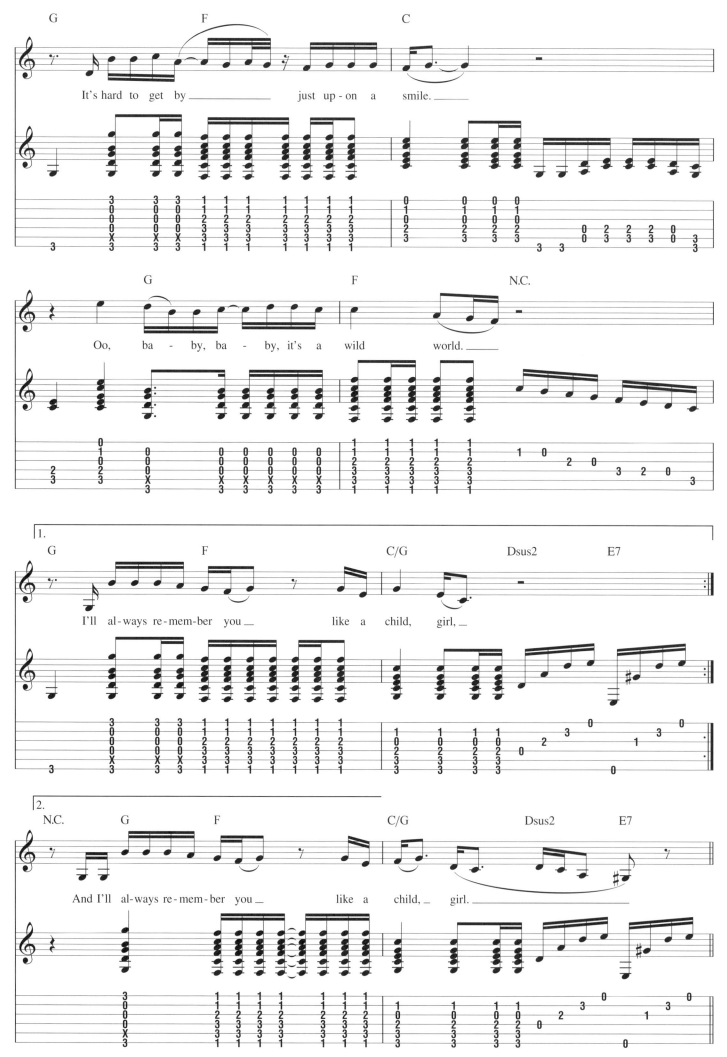

Well,   oo, ba - by, ba - by, it's a wild   world. __

It's hard to get by _____   just up - on a   smile. __

Oo,   ba - by, ba - by, it's a   wild   world. _____

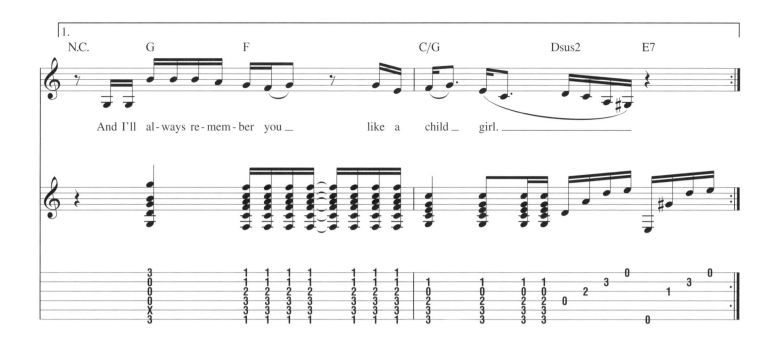

And I'll al-ways re-mem-ber you _ like a child _ girl. _____

And I'll al-ways re-mem-ber you _ like a child, girl. _____

Additional Lyrics

2. You know I've seen a lot of what the world can do
   And it's breakin' my heart in two
   Because I never want to see you sad, girl. Don't be a bad girl.
   But if you want to leave, take good care.
   Hope you make a lot of nice friends out there,
   But just remember there's a lot of bad and beware.

This series will help you play your favorite songs quickly and easily. Just follow the tab and listen to the CD to hear how the guitar should sound, and then play along using the separate backing tracks. Mac or PC users can also slow down the tempo without changing pitch by using the CD in their computer. The melody and lyrics are included in the book so that you can sing or simply follow along.

INCLUDES TAB

1. ROCK
00699570 ....$16.99

2. ACOUSTIC
00699569.................$16.95

3. HARD ROCK
00699573.................$16.95

4. POP/ROCK
00699571.................$16.99

5. MODERN ROCK
00699574 ....$16.99

6. '90s ROCK
00699572.................$16.99

7. BLUES
00699575.................$16.95

8. ROCK
00699585.................$14.99

9. PUNK ROCK
00699576.................$14.95

10. ACOUSTIC
00699586.................$16.95

11. EARLY ROCK
0699579.................$14.95

12. POP/ROCK
00699587.................$14.95

13. FOLK ROCK
00699581.................$14.95

14. BLUES ROCK
00699582.................$16.95

15. R&B
00699583.................$14.95

16. JAZZ
00699584.................$15.95

17. COUNTRY
00699588.................$15.95

18. ACOUSTIC ROCK
00699577.................$15.95

19. SOUL
00699578.................$14.99

20. ROCKABILLY
00699580.................$14.95

21. YULETIDE
00699602.................$14.95

22. CHRISTMAS
00699600.................$15.95

23. SURF
00699635.................$14.95

24. ERIC CLAPTON
00699649.................$17.99

25. LENNON & McCARTNEY
00699642 ....$16.99

26. ELVIS PRESLEY
00699643.................$14.95

27. DAVID LEE ROTH
00699645.................$16.95

28. GREG KOCH
00699646.................$14.95

29. BOB SEGER
00699647.................$15.99

30. KISS
00699644.................$16.99

31. CHRISTMAS HITS
00699652.................$14.95

32. THE OFFSPRING
00699653.................$14.95

33. ACOUSTIC CLASSICS
00699656.................$16.95

34. CLASSIC ROCK
00699658.................$16.95

35. HAIR METAL
00699660.................$16.95

36. SOUTHERN ROCK
00699661.................$16.95

37. ACOUSTIC METAL
00699662.................$16.95

38. BLUES
00699663.................$16.95

39. '80s METAL
00699664.................$16.99

40. INCUBUS
00699668.................$17.95

41. ERIC CLAPTON
00699669.................$16.95

42. 2000s ROCK
00699670.................$16.99

43. LYNYRD SKYNYRD
00699681.................$17.95

44. JAZZ
00699689.................$14.99

45. TV THEMES
00699718.................$14.95

46. MAINSTREAM ROCK
00699722.................$16.95

47. HENDRIX SMASH HITS
00699723.................$19.95

48. AEROSMITH CLASSICS
00699724.................$17.99

49. STEVIE RAY VAUGHAN
00699725.................$17.99

50. 2000s METAL
00699726.................$16.99

51. ALTERNATIVE '90s
00699727.................$12.95

52. FUNK
00699728.................$14.95

53. DISCO
00699729.................$14.99

54. HEAVY METAL
00699730.................$14.95

55. POP METAL
00699731.................$14.95

56. FOO FIGHTERS
00699749.................$14.95

57. SYSTEM OF A DOWN
00699751.................$14.95

58. BLINK-182
00699772.................$14.95

60. 3 DOORS DOWN
00699774.................$14.95

61. SLIPKNOT
00699775.................$14.95

62. CHRISTMAS CAROLS
00699798.................$12.95

63. CREEDENCE CLEARWATER REVIVAL
00699802.................$16.99

64. OZZY OSBOURNE
00699803.................$16.99

65. THE DOORS
00699806.................$16.99

66. THE ROLLING STONES 00699807.....................$16.95	**87. ACOUSTIC WOMEN** 00700763 ....$14.99	**111. JOHN MELLENCAMP** 00701056 ....$14.99	**128. 1960s ROCK** 00701740....................$14.99
67. BLACK SABBATH 00699808.....................$16.99	**88. GRUNGE** 00700467 ....$16.99	**112. QUEEN** 00701052 ....$16.99	**129. MEGADETH** 00701741....................$14.99
68. PINK FLOYD – DARK SIDE OF THE MOON 00699809.....................$16.99	**90. CLASSICAL POP** 00700469....................$12.99	**113. JIM CROCE** 00701058 ....$14.99	**130. IRON MAIDEN** 00701742....................$16.99
69. ACOUSTIC FAVORITES 00699810.....................$14.95	**91. BLUES INSTRUMENTALS** 00700505 ....$14.99	**114. BON JOVI** 00701060 ....$14.99	**131. 1990s ROCK** 00701743....................$14.99
70. OZZY OSBOURNE 00699805.....................$16.99	**92. EARLY ROCK INSTRUMENTALS** 00700506 ....$12.99	**115. JOHNNY CASH** 00701070 ....$16.99	**132. COUNTRY ROCK** 00701757 ....$14.99
71. CHRISTIAN ROCK 00699824.....................$14.95	**93. ROCK INSTRUMENTALS** 00700507 ....$16.99	**116. THE VENTURES** 00701124 ....$14.99	**133. TAYLOR SWIFT** 00701894 ....$16.99
72. ACOUSTIC '90s 00699827.....................$14.95	**95. BLUES CLASSICS** 00700509 ....$14.99	**119. AC/DC CLASSICS** 00701356 ....$17.99	**134. AVENGED SEVENFOLD** 00701906 ....$16.99
73. BLUESY ROCK 00699829 ....$16.99	**96. THIRD DAY** 00700560 ....$14.95	**120. PROGRESSIVE ROCK** 00701457....................$14.99	**136. GUITAR THEMES** 00701922 ....$14.99
74. PAUL BALOCHE 00699831....................$14.95	**97. ROCK BAND** 00700703....................$14.99	**121. U2** 00701508 ....$16.99	**139. GARY MOORE** 00702370 ....$16.99
75. TOM PETTY 00699882.....................$16.99	**98. ROCK BAND** 00700704....................$14.95	**122. CROSBY, STILLS & NASH** 00701610....................$16.99	**141. ACOUSTIC HITS** 00702401 ....$16.99
76. COUNTRY HITS 00699884.....................$14.95	**99. ZZ TOP** 00700762 ....$16.99	**123. LENNON & McCARTNEY ACOUSTIC** 00701614....................$16.99	**142. KINGS OF LEON** 00702418 ....$16.99
77. BLUEGRASS 00699910.....................$12.99	**100. B.B. KING** 00700466 ....$14.99	**124. MODERN WORSHIP** 00701629....................$14.99	**145. DEF LEPPARD** 00702532 ....$16.99
78. NIRVANA 00700132.....................$16.99	**101. SONGS FOR BEGINNERS** 00701917 ....$14.99	**125. JEFF BECK** 00701687 ....$16.99	**149. AC/DC HITS** 14041593 ....$17.99
88. ACOUSTIC ANTHOLOGY 00700175.....................$19.95	**102. CLASSIC PUNK** 00700769....................$14.99	**126. BOB MARLEY** 00701701....................$16.99	
81. ROCK ANTHOLOGY 00700176.....................$22.99	**103. SWITCHFOOT** 00700773 ....$16.99	**127. 1970s ROCK** 00701739....................$14.99	
82. EASY ROCK SONGS 00700177.....................$12.99	**104. DUANE ALLMAN** 00700846....................$16.99		
83. THREE CHORD SONGS 00700178....................$16.99	**106. WEEZER** 00700958 ....$14.99		
84. STEELY DAN 00700200 ....$16.99	**107. CREAM** 00701069....................$16.99		
85. THE POLICE 00700269 ....$16.99	**108. THE WHO** 00701053 ....$16.99		
86. BOSTON 00700465 ....$16.99	**109. STEVE MILLER** 00701054 ....$14.99		

HAL•LEONARD® CORPORATION

7777 W. BLUEMOUND RD. P.O. BOX 13819 MILWAUKEE, WI 53213

For complete songlists, visit Hal Leonard online at
www.halleonard.com

Prices, contents, and availability subject to change without notice.

RECORDED VERSIONS®

The Best Note-For-Note Transcriptions Available

ALL BOOKS INCLUDE TABLATURE

14037551 AC/DC – Backtracks	$32.99	
00692015 Aerosmith – Greatest Hits	$22.95	
00690178 Alice in Chains – Acoustic	$19.95	
00694865 Alice in Chains – Dirt	$19.95	
00690812 All American Rejects – Move Along	$19.95	
00690958 Duane Allman Guitar Anthology	$24.99	
00694932 Allman Brothers Band – Volume 1	$24.95	
00694933 Allman Brothers Band – Volume 2	$24.95	
00694934 Allman Brothers Band – Volume 3	$24.95	
00690865 Atreyu – A Deathgrip on Yesterday	$19.95	
00690609 Audioslave	$19.95	
00690820 Avenged Sevenfold – City of Evil	$24.95	
00690366 Bad Company – Original Anthology	$19.95	
00690503 Beach Boys – Very Best of	$19.95	
00690489 Beatles – 1	$24.99	
00694832 Beatles – For Acoustic Guitar	$22.99	
00691014 Beatles Rock Band	$34.99	
00690110 Beatles – White Album (Book 1)	$19.95	
00691043 Jeff Beck – Wired	$19.99	
00692385 Chuck Berry	$19.95	
00690835 Billy Talent	$19.95	
00690901 Best of Black Sabbath	$19.95	
00690831 blink-182 – Greatest Hits	$19.95	
00690913 Boston	$19.95	
00690932 Boston – Don't Look Back	$19.99	
00690491 David Bowie – Best of	$19.95	
00690873 Breaking Benjamin – Phobia	$19.95	
00690451 Jeff Buckley – Collection	$24.95	
00690957 Bullet for My Valentine – Scream Aim Fire	$19.95	
00691004 Chickenfoot	$22.99	
00690590 Eric Clapton – Anthology	$29.95	
00690415 Clapton Chronicles – Best of Eric Clapton	$18.95	
00690936 Eric Clapton – Complete Clapton	$29.99	
00690074 Eric Clapton – The Cream of Clapton	$24.95	
00694869 Eric Clapton – Unplugged	$22.95	
00690162 The Clash – Best of	$19.95	
00690828 Coheed & Cambria – Good Apollo I'm Burning Star, IV, Vol. 1: From Fear Through the Eyes of Madness	$19.95	
00690593 Coldplay – A Rush of Blood to the Head	$19.95	
00690962 Coldplay – Viva La Vida	$19.95	
00690819 Creedence Clearwater Revival – Best of	$22.95	
00690648 The Very Best of Jim Croce	$19.95	
00690613 Crosby, Stills & Nash – Best of	$22.95	
00690967 Death Cab for Cutie – Narrow Stairs	$22.99	
00690289 Deep Purple – Best of	$17.95	
00690784 Def Leppard – Best of	$19.95	
00692240 Bo Diddley	$19.99	
00690347 The Doors – Anthology	$22.95	
00690348 The Doors – Essential Guitar Collection	$16.95	
00690810 Fall Out Boy – From Under the Cork Tree	$19.95	
00690664 Fleetwood Mac – Best of	$19.95	
00690870 Flyleaf	$19.95	
00690931 Foo Fighters – Echoes, Silence, Patience & Grace	$19.95	
00690808 Foo Fighters – In Your Honor	$19.95	
00690805 Robben Ford – Best of	$19.95	
00694920 Free – Best of	$19.95	
00691050 Glee Guitar Collection	$19.99	
00690848 Godsmack – IV	$19.95	
00690943 The Goo Goo Dolls – Greatest Hits Volume 1: The Singles	$22.95	
00701764 Guitar Tab White Pages – Play-Along	$39.99	
00694854 Buddy Guy – Damn Right, I've Got the Blues	$19.95	

00690840 Ben Harper – Both Sides of the Gun	$19.95	
00694798 George Harrison – Anthology	$19.95	
00690841 Scott Henderson – Blues Guitar Collection	$19.95	
00692930 Jimi Hendrix – Are You Experienced?	$24.95	
00692931 Jimi Hendrix – Axis: Bold As Love	$22.95	
00692932 Jimi Hendrix – Electric Ladyland	$24.95	
00690017 Jimi Hendrix – Live at Woodstock	$24.95	
00690602 Jimi Hendrix – Smash Hits	$24.99	
00690793 John Lee Hooker Anthology	$24.99	
00690692 Billy Idol – Very Best of	$19.95	
00690688 Incubus – A Crow Left of the Murder	$19.95	
00690544 Incubus – Morningview	$19.95	
00690790 Iron Maiden Anthology	$24.99	
00690721 Jet – Get Born	$19.95	
00690684 Jethro Tull – Aqualung	$19.95	
00690959 John5 – Requiem	$22.95	
00690814 John5 – Songs for Sanity	$19.95	
00690751 John5 – Vertigo	$19.95	
00690845 Eric Johnson – Bloom	$19.95	
00690846 Jack Johnson and Friends – Sing-A-Longs and Lullabies for the Film Curious George	$19.95	
00690271 Robert Johnson – New Transcriptions	$24.95	
00699131 Janis Joplin – Best of	$19.95	
00690427 Judas Priest – Best of	$22.99	
00690742 The Killers – Hot Fuss	$19.95	
00690975 Kings of Leon – Only by the Night	$22.99	
00694903 Kiss – Best of	$24.95	
00690355 Kiss – Destroyer	$16.95	
00690834 Lamb of God – Ashes of the Wake	$19.95	
00690875 Lamb of God – Sacrament	$19.95	
00690823 Ray LaMontagne – Trouble	$19.95	
00690679 John Lennon – Guitar Collection	$19.95	
00690781 Linkin Park – Hybrid Theory	$22.95	
00690743 Los Lonely Boys	$19.95	
00690720 Lostprophets – Start Something	$19.95	
00690955 Lynyrd Skynyrd – All-Time Greatest Hits	$19.99	
00694954 Lynyrd Skynyrd – New Best of	$19.95	
00690754 Marilyn Manson – Lest We Forget	$19.95	
00694956 Bob Marley– Legend	$19.95	
00694945 Bob Marley– Songs of Freedom	$24.95	
00690657 Maroon5 – Songs About Jane	$19.95	
00120080 Don McLean – Songbook	$19.95	
00694951 Megadeth – Rust in Peace	$22.95	
00690951 Megadeth – United Abominations	$22.99	
00690505 John Mellencamp – Guitar Collection	$19.95	
00690646 Pat Metheny – One Quiet Night	$19.95	
00690558 Pat Metheny – Trio: 99>00	$19.95	
00690040 Steve Miller Band – Young Hearts	$19.95	
00694883 Nirvana – Nevermind	$19.95	
00690026 Nirvana – Unplugged in New York	$19.95	
00690807 The Offspring – Greatest Hits	$19.95	
00694847 Ozzy Osbourne – Best of	$22.95	
00690399 Ozzy Osbourne – Ozzman Cometh	$22.99	
00690933 Best of Brad Paisley	$22.95	
00690995 Brad Paisley – Play: The Guitar Album	$24.99	
00690866 Panic! At the Disco – A Fever You Can't Sweat Out	$19.95	
00690938 Christopher Parkening – Duets & Concertos	$24.99	
00694855 Pearl Jam – Ten	$19.95	
00690439 A Perfect Circle – Mer De Noms	$19.95	
00690499 Tom Petty – Definitive Guitar Collection	$19.95	
00690428 Pink Floyd – Dark Side of the Moon	$19.95	
00690789 Poison – Best of	$19.95	
00693864 The Police – Best of	$19.95	

00694975 Queen – Greatest Hits	$24.95	
00690670 Queensryche – Very Best of	$19.95	
00690878 The Raconteurs – Broken Boy Soldiers	$19.95	
00694910 Rage Against the Machine	$19.95	
00690055 Red Hot Chili Peppers – Blood Sugar Sex Magik	$19.95	
00690584 Red Hot Chili Peppers – By the Way	$19.95	
00690852 Red Hot Chili Peppers –Stadium Arcadium	$24.95	
00690511 Django Reinhardt – Definitive Collection	$19.95	
00690779 Relient K – MMHMM	$19.95	
00690631 Rolling Stones – Guitar Anthology	$27.95	
00694976 Rolling Stones – Some Girls	$22.95	
00690264 The Rolling Stones – Tattoo You	$19.95	
00690685 David Lee Roth – Eat 'Em and Smile	$19.95	
00690942 David Lee Roth and the Songs of Van Halen	$19.95	
00690031 Santana's Greatest Hits	$19.95	
00690566 Scorpions – Best of	$22.95	
00690604 Bob Seger – Guitar Collection	$19.95	
00690803 Kenny Wayne Shepherd Band – Best of	$19.95	
00690968 Shinedown – The Sound of Madness	$22.99	
00690813 Slayer – Guitar Collection	$19.95	
00690733 Slipknot – Vol. 3 (The Subliminal Verses)	$22.99	
00120004 Steely Dan – Best of	$24.95	
00694921 Steppenwolf – Best of	$22.95	
00690655 Mike Stern – Best of	$19.95	
00690877 Stone Sour – Come What(ever) May	$19.95	
00690520 Styx Guitar Collection	$19.95	
00120081 Sublime	$19.95	
00120122 Sublime – 40oz. to Freedom	$19.95	
00690929 Sum 41 – Underclass Hero	$19.95	
00690767 Switchfoot – The Beautiful Letdown	$19.95	
00690993 Taylor Swift – Fearless	$22.99	
00690830 System of a Down – Hypnotize	$19.95	
00690799 System of a Down – Mezmerize	$19.95	
00690531 System of a Down – Toxicity	$19.95	
00694824 James Taylor – Best of	$16.95	
00690871 Three Days Grace – One-X	$19.95	
00690737 3 Doors Down – The Better Life	$22.95	
00690683 Robin Trower – Bridge of Sighs	$19.95	
00699191 U2 – Best of: 1980-1990	$19.95	
00690732 U2 – Best of: 1990-2000	$19.95	
00660137 Steve Vai – Passion & Warfare	$24.95	
00690116 Stevie Ray Vaughan – Guitar Collection	$24.95	
00660058 Stevie Ray Vaughan – Lightnin' Blues 1983-1987	$24.95	
00694835 Stevie Ray Vaughan – The Sky Is Crying	$22.95	
00690015 Stevie Ray Vaughan – Texas Flood	$19.95	
00690772 Velvet Revolver – Contraband	$22.95	
00690071 Weezer (The Blue Album)	$19.95	
00690966 Weezer – (Red Album)	$19.99	
00690447 The Who – Best of	$24.95	
00690916 The Best of Dwight Yoakam	$19.95	
00690905 Neil Young – Rust Never Sleeps	$19.99	
00690623 Frank Zappa – Over-Nite Sensation	$22.99	
00690589 ZZ Top Guitar Anthology	$24.95	

Prices and availability subject to change without notice. Some products may not be available outside the U.S.A.

0211